The Well Trained Puppy: Housebreaking, Commands to Shape Behavior and All Training Needed for a Happy, Obedient Dog

By Faye Dunningham

ISBN-13: 978-1479207237

ISBN-10: 1479207233

A B C Chags Publishing

Table of Contents

Why Training is Important and How it Shapes Your Dog's Personality

Every loving owner wishes to have a well-trained, well behaved dog. The two most crucial elements are housetraining and command training.

While one answer to "Why housetrain?" is obvious, there are other reasons as well. Despite being domesticated for over ten thousand years, today's canine family members still carry very strong instinct that has been retained over all of this time. One strong instinct that dogs have is the desire to have structure.

Most owners have heard of a dog's need to live in a "pack". Long ago in the wild, a dog's pack consisted of the other dogs that he ran with. Dogs stayed together in packs for survival purposes. They would hunt together and offer each other protection from the many dangers that existed as they roamed in search of food and shelter.

In today's world, your dog's pack is his human family and any other household pets. This pack has an "Alpha" who is the leader. This ranking should be held by the owner(s) but sometimes it can be the dog and this must be corrected. This holds true for a small household with one dog and one owner...And it holds true for large households with many people and multiple pets.

When living in a pack (your family), your dog will assume that he will have structure. Structure will include a daily routine. The daily routine will include all of the basic elements that make up your dog's day. Part of this should include going to the bathroom in a designated area.

Dogs that have this structure, knowing what to expect and have been taught where and when to expect it, feel more at peace. There are less "unknowns" and this creates a feeling of security and safety. This in turn, is one of the elements that will lead to an owner having a better-behaved dog.

Behavior is fundamentally affected by both housetraining and command training.

Without proper housetraining and proper command training, a dog is essentially allowed to do as he pleases. Without this training, owners may still feel as if they are in charge since they feed their dog and supply a home to their dog. *However, if a dog is not trained to listen, this is the same as the dog being taught that he does not need to listen.*

When a dog is taught that he does not need to listen and may do as he pleases, a dog perceives this as a clear message that *he* is in charge (the Alpha).

Living in the pack and being told that he is in charge (from a lack of proper training), that dog will not only do as he pleases, he will also behave in a way that can lead to total chaos. An improperly trained dog can become a nipper, a biter, a beggar, a barker and/or display destructive behavior both in the home and/or around the neighborhood.

An improperly trained dog will walk the owner instead of the owner walking him. He will strut around the home and outside property believing that he is the leader of the pack (the Alpha) and this does not make for a happy, peaceful household.

Not only is this an undesirable living situation for an owner, it is also not desirable for a dog. Domesticated dogs, that are mistakenly taught that they hold the Alpha position, have a great deal of stress on them. Taking on the role of the Alpha, they are always on guard and always "readied" to protect and to make decisions.

If, however, a dog is properly housetrained and trained in commands, this moves the balance of power over to the owner. When this happens, the weight of being the Alpha is not put on a dog. This allows him to relax and feel secure that his human is taking care of him. He will then be able to understand and importantly, *allow* himself to follow commands and display behaviors that his humans desire for him to display. The dog is at peace and the owner is the Alpha of a content household in which the dog is well mannered.

Another issue that can come into play is that a dog may be "taught" two different lessons at the same time. When his owner feeds him (in the proper way), this sends a clear message that the owner is the Alpha.

Simultaneously, if the dog is "taught" that he is in charge due to a lack of training, he is then given a contradictory message that *he* is the Alpha.

The constant opposing messages create an inner battle in a dog's mind. He is now unsure of his status. He continually questions, "Am I the Alpha? Is my human the Alpha?" There can *never* be two Alphas...And a dog will not rest until he finds the answer.

This can create a power struggle between dog and owner. The dog, ruled by raw canine instinct, will test and challenge his possible Alpha position. Therefore, an improperly trained dog that has no idea who the Alpha is, since a lack of training did not instill the answer, will often *not* have consistent good behavior. Essentially, chaos can set in as he struggles to find out what his position is.

Finally, training (specifically command training) allows an owner to enjoy the true benefits of having a canine family member. For example, it is sad sight to see owners who think that they are walking their dog, when in fact the dog is in charge. Surely you have seen this or perhaps you are experiencing this...The dog walks ahead of the owner. The dog stops when he wishes and runs ahead when he desires. The leash is taut and the owner lags behind.

It is an unfortunate situation when owners do not realize what is happening. They may feel that since they are outside with the dog and *technically* the two are walking that this fits the description of "walking the dog". It does not. The dog is walking on his own and is only limited by the length of the leash, which the dog interprets as an irritation and not a method of guidance by his leader.

When a dog heels while walking, both owner and dog walk in tandem with a clear mutual understanding that the owner is in charge of both speed and direction. Just this one element alone creates so much more pleasure when out for daily walks. An owner can then walk proudly and when in the "Heeling" position, dogs of all ages walk just as proudly as owners do.

 Taking your dog for a 20 minute walk each day is proven to:

- **Reduce a dog's pent up energy that can be otherwise directed toward destructive behavior**
- **Helps to keep a dog agile and limber**
- **Reduces digestive problems**
- **Helps a dog maintain a healthy weight**

Even the basic commands of "Sit" and "Stay" have a great impact on behavior. For any dog that has an inappropriate reaction to a physical trigger or a social situation, commanding that dog to "Sit" and then "Stay" can allow the dog to gain composure.

While socialization training may be needed for overly fearful, shy or aggressive puppies, commands play a huge role. When a puppy is fully trained for commands, there will then be procedures in place that guide that puppy toward displaying more appropriate behavior.

Just as importantly, a dog gains self-confidence when he learns commands. And this plays a huge role in his personality. Just as a human's personality gradually changes over time as he learns new skills, meets new people and gains life experience, so does a dog's personality.

Opposite to how a dog will cower down and feel anxious and dejected if yelled at or mistreated, a dog that is being praised and rewarded for following commands will carry himself with pride and have a happier disposition.

Obedience training is the hallmark of a well-behaved, well-mannered dog. A dog that sits, stays and comes to you on command is showing refined behavior and displaying gracious intelligence.

Now that we have discussed why training is so important for both owner and dog, we will go into detail regarding the most challenging training: housetraining.

Housetraining

Important Elements to Keep in Mind Before You Begin

Your Puppy's Ability

To begin, let's discuss the requirements that a puppy has in regard to urination and bowel elimination (how often these bodily functions will happen) and the capability to hold them (the limit of how long a puppy can hold back  the need to expel urine and bowel movements).

After all, you cannot expect a puppy to do something that he literally cannot do. When you understand what your puppy *can* do, you will know what expectations are reasonable.

When a puppy is born, he has very little control over bladder and bowel muscles. When a puppy is a newborn, control over these muscles is *so* limited that the dam (the puppy's mother) often must stimulate the puppy's body to expel bowel movements. She often does this by licking the outside of the puppy's anus. The stimulation triggers the nerves in the rectum which results in a bowel movement.

In regard to urination, the bladder is a hollow muscle. It fills with urine and it swells in the process. Below a puppy's bladder are sphincter muscles. These sphincter muscles keep urine from leaking out. As a newborn, the sphincter muscles are very weak. Therefore, it is common for urine to simply leak out before the bladder is completely full.

Each week, the bowel muscles and the sphincter muscles gain strength. This will naturally happen on its own; however a very important element for owners to know is that a puppy often cannot gain full control over these muscles without some help.

By the time an owner obtains a puppy, with that puppy normally being eight weeks old, the puppy has naturally gained some strength in both sphincter muscles and bowel muscles. However, a puppy is not even close to having full control.

It is vital to understand a puppy's limitations and then to housetrain with that in mind. Success or failure will depend greatly on knowing how long a puppy can realistically hold in urine and feces. Before we move on to that, do keep in mind that each month there *can be* a marked increase in time that a puppy can hold his needs; and when properly housetraining you will play a role in helping your puppy gain that strength.

In regard to urination, in general, an 8 week old puppy can hold his needs for 2 hours. A 3 month old can hold his needs for approximately 3 hours. A 4 month old can hold his needs for approximately 4 hours and so on. Once a puppy reaches the age of 8 months old and is capable of holding his needs for 8 hours, the time often does not exceed this.

In some cases, an adult dog may hold his needs for 9 or even perhaps 10 hours, however this puts a great deal of both physical and emotional stress on a dog. When properly trained, a dog knows that he pleases his owner only when eliminating in a designated area and a dog may exert great control, and some may even endure pain, in an effort to not eliminate in the house. It is not fair to place a dog in a pressure-filled situation such as this.

In regard to bowel movements, a young puppy usually has frequent bowel movements. There are two main reasons for this. First, when properly fed, a puppy is free-feeding until the age of 3 months old. Free-feeding is the method of leaving out a constant supply of fresh food. This is highly suggested for any puppy until he reaches the age of 3 months old, since even going without food for a few hours can cause hypoglycemia. Hypoglycemia is a rapid drop in blood sugar levels and this can be fatal.

From the age of 3 months to anywhere between 6 months and 1 year, a puppy is eating 3 times per day. Snacks are often given in addition to this (and are needed when command training).

Therefore eating throughout the day often causes a puppy's body to have more than one bowel movement. Please never limit food or refrain from giving treats when command training in a misguided attempt to decrease the need for bowel movements; doing so would be to put your puppy's health in great jeopardy.

Secondly, a young puppy's entire digestive system runs faster than that of an older, adult dog. Food is processed quickly and within 15 to 20 minutes after eating a puppy may need to eliminate. Remember that as each day and week goes by, a puppy will be able to hold his needs for longer and longer periods of time. A young puppy may need to be brought outside many times during the day and night; but this is a temporary phase.

Keeping in mind the capabilities of a puppy in regard to urination needs and bowel movements, part of being a loving owner is to understand the very real limitations of a puppy or dog and then setup a schedule that fits those very real limitations and not just what you desire them to be. To expect a puppy to hold on for longer than is physically possible is a sure road to disaster.

How a Puppy Learns

A puppy has absolutely no idea that he is supposed to urinate or eliminate where you want him to. For a young puppy with very little muscle control, urinating or eliminating next to your sofa, right near the front door or outside are all the same unless he is taught otherwise.

Very importantly, yelling or showing frustration when a puppy urinates or eliminates in an undesired location holds *zero* weight in housetraining a puppy. Based off of any words of frustration or negative tone of voice a puppy *may* learn that he did something undesirable...But it does *not* teach him what *is* desired.

Only if a puppy receives praise and treats after taking a certain action, will he ultimately learn that he did something "right" and that his human is happy. When done properly, a puppy will reach a moment of realizing that going potty in a certain location brings benefits: treats, praise and attention. *After this,* treats do *not* need to be given, as the desired actions will become automated behavior. It is then that a dog is fully trained.

Another element to keep in mind is that housetraining must be done consistently. This means that if you stick to the rules one day, but do not follow them the next, all that you will have is one confused puppy. Alternatively, if you follow the housetraining rules when you are home but another family member does not follow them when he or she is in charge of the puppy, again you will have a very confused puppy.

Think about how you would feel if you were told by local authorities to park your car in the street. Wanting to do the right thing, you did so, only to be told the next day that you can park anywhere you wish. You then decide to park in your driveway, only to be yelled at that you didn't park in the garage. You would end up feeling very stressed and confused. Every time you had to park your car, you would have no idea what was expected. It would not be too long before you decided just to park wherever you wished since you were receiving mixed signals regardless.

This is what will happen if a puppy does not receive continual, consistent housetraining. Only when he is repeatedly shown what is to be expected and he receives praise for doing so, will a puppy learn what to do.

Your Big Decision

First, you will need to decide if you will be housetraining indoors or outdoors. While some toy and small breed dogs are able to be housetrained indoors on pee-pads, this indoor method takes much longer for a puppy to learn. All dogs, no matter which breed, have a deep canine instinct to eliminate outdoors. They have an urge to walk around their territory, to sniff for the scent of other dogs and animals and finally choose "just the right spot".

When an owner's goal is for a puppy to urinate and eliminate indoors on pee-pads or newspaper, this creates a barrier that a dog must then conquer. It goes against his canine nature; he is not allowed to choose his spot and this not only can be stressful but it is a path to a much longer housetraining process.

It will be important to choose one method and to stick to that method. If you choose the recommended outdoor training, there may be times when you are not home and the situation requires the use of pee-pads. Take into account that the pee-pads will be temporary. As your puppy grows and gains bowel and sphincter muscle strength, with your help he will work his way up to being able to hold his needs when you are not home and ultimately only going to the bathroom outside.

Keeping all of this in mind, you may be in a situation that dictates indoor training. If this is the case, do not despair. While indoor training often takes longer than outdoor training, it can be done. Since outdoor training is recommended we will go over the details of that first, followed by indoor training.

The Detailed Process of Housetraining Outdoors

Can a Puppy Come to You Already Housebroken?

Some breeders will claim that they sell puppies that are already housebroken, or at least well on their way to being housebroken. While they may be correct in one sense, this rarely relates to the definition of housetraining that you will have. This is because, for those breeders who claim this, many put down newspaper in small enclosed areas and when the puppy has no other choice but to urinate or eliminate on them, this is perceived as a sort of "housebreaking". It is not.

Another situation in which a breeder may claim that a puppy is housebroken is when the breeder has the dam in the home along with a litter of puppies. When the puppies reach the age of approximately six weeks old, they often follow their mother around. When the mother goes outside for her bathroom needs, the puppies may trot along right behind her and then copy her actions.

If these were the circumstances, the puppy was taking *action by example*. Once separated from the dam and littermates, that same puppy will often have no concept of actual housetraining. Therefore, even if your puppy was "housetrained" by a breeder, you most likely will need to disregard that claim and proceed with all of the following steps.

Choosing an Area

One of the most important elements of housetraining is to choose one area for your dog's urination and elimination needs.  Thought should be put into this decision. If you live in a location in which you have different weather seasons, think about how accessible the location will be not only on nice sunny days but also when there is rain or deep snow.

The designated area should be for urination and elimination needs only. You will not want the area to be one in which your puppy plays. It should not be an area of high foot traffic and it should not be right next to your outdoor grill, etc. It does not need to be an overly large area, but simply one that is separate from anything else. A space of even ten feet by ten feet is sufficient.

Rules to Always Follow When Going to the Designated Area

While you will choose the area, your puppy should be allowed to choose "just the right spot". Even if the area that you have chosen is a small enclosed area, your puppy should always be brought out on a leash. This is very important for successful housetraining. At all times, you should have control and that is best done with the use of a leash.

Any time that you bring your puppy out to go to the bathroom, you should put a small and tasty treat into your pocket. It is best if your puppy does not see the treat. It usually works well to have several stashes of treats in various rooms of the home so that if you must rush out, you will still be able to quickly grab one before exiting.

Each time that you bring your puppy out, you should exit the home first. Exiting the home first is part of training your puppy that you are the Alpha. (Full "Alpha Training" is ahead in a following chapter). Therefore, you will put the leash on your puppy, exit first and head directly to the designed area.

Do not make any stops on the way. For example, do not go to the mailbox and then head to the designated area. Also, do not play with your puppy. This is because when you bring your puppy outside for bathroom needs, it is a serious time. This means no throwing around a ball, no stopping to allow your puppy to sniff around any other area on the way, no talking other than key words and praise and no distractions. This will allow him to fully focus on the task at hand.

Dogs can sense odors at concentrations approximately 100 million times lower than humans can. Therefore when you take your puppy outside, his senses are being bombarded with all sorts of odors. Understanding this, you will need to take charge in leading him to the designated area...Otherwise your dog would be happy to spend an hour sniffing around.

If you are heading to the designated area because your puppy showed signs of needing to go to the bathroom (more on this ahead), you will repeat a key word as you walk him there. You may choose "Bathroom", "Potty", or any other word of your choosing that will always be applied when he urinates or eliminates.

If your puppy did not show signs, but you are bringing him based on the schedule (more ahead), you will not say that key word, as it will be reserved for when he actually urinates or eliminates.

When you lead your puppy to the area, it is best to have him on a six foot leash. Once you reach the designated area, you will stand in the middle of that area. The puppy should be allowed to roam around within the perimeter that you have established by positioning yourself right in the center.

One of the most common reasons for failure in housetraining is the patience level of an owner. Countless owners complain that their puppy goes to the bathroom right after coming back in the house. Usually this is because the owner did not have the patience to wait for the puppy's body to release urine or push out feces as it can take longer than one may think.

While puppies may have times of immediately relieving themselves, most need 5 to 15 minutes to do so. This is especially relevant in regard to bowel movements. Rarely will a puppy have feces in the rectum, just waiting to be quickly released. It takes time for a puppy to learn how to control his muscles and push out feces.

For this reason and to find a fast road to success, have patience. Some owners find that they can offer this important element by leaving an outdoor chair in the middle of the designated area and sitting down as opposed to standing. This is especially helpful if it is raining or if an owner tends to feel antsy after a couple of minutes.

If your puppy tries to play with you or gain your attention, nicely ignore him. If you allow him to become distracted by playing with him or engaging him, he will forget about his needs and opt instead to play. Playtime and attention can be part of his reward once he has gone to the bathroom. Therefore, using a timer or watch, wait at least 15 minutes and have that time be spent only with your puppy being allowed to go to the bathroom if he needs to.

If your puppy is urinating or eliminating in the area, as he is doing so, repeat the key word of "Bathroom", "Potty" or any other word that you have chosen to communicate to your puppy that his actions have a word and that you are recognizing what he is doing. Use a happy, enthusiastic tone of voice.

 The average dog understands 165 words...Therefore when you reinforce a word such as "Potty", this is not done in vain. Your puppy will learn this word and many others!

As soon as your puppy is done, immediately give him the treat that you have brought with you and offer great words of praise. Be sure to say, "Good Potty!" to help your puppy connect his actions to the key word of "potty". You may then also follow with "Good Boy!" or "Good Girl!" When you say these words of praise, you will want to make him feel as if he just did the most wonderful thing in the entire world.

If your puppy does not go to the bathroom, do not immediately begin playing with him. Bring him back inside, wait approximately five minutes and then play if you wish. If you play with him right away, he may interpret this as meaning that if he walks to the designated area and simply waits a while, it will lead to a fun play session. Therefore, waiting a small amount of time separates the two events and does not create misinterpretation.

If your puppy has indeed gone to the bathroom, with praise and a treat being given immediately afterward, you can now feel free to play outdoors with your puppy (just not very near to that designated bathroom area!) or continue on with any other activities.

If you are planning to take your puppy for a walk, it is best to encourage him to go to the bathroom first before you begin walking. If you are walking your puppy and he stops along the way to go to the bathroom, this is a missed opportunity to teach him to use the designated area. It is best to first bring him out for the 15 minutes first and then if he does not need to go, proceed with the walk.

If he did *not* go to the bathroom before or during the walk, do not enter back into the home without a stop at the designated area. Chances are that a puppy will go potty in the chosen area either before or after a walk if given the opportunity.

When to Bring Your Puppy Out

As discussed earlier, your puppy will only be able to hold his urination needs for a certain amount of hours, based on his age. This should be the first element of your schedule.

Unless another reason comes up for going to the designated area, you will want to bring him there every 2 hours for a 2 month old, every 3 hours for a 3 month old, every 4 hours for a 4 month old, etc. until a puppy is 8 months old or older and at the 8 hour mark.

The exception will be during the night, which will be discussed ahead.

Aside from this, you will want to bring your puppy to the designated area every morning as soon as he wakes up. This should be done immediately before any other task or activity is done. You will want to also bring him there as soon as he wakes up from any naps. Your final time to bring him out will be right before bedtime.

For bowel movements, you will want to bring your puppy outside 15 to 20 minutes after eating. In many cases, a puppy will urinate first and then if allowed to remain in the designated area, after 5 to 10 minutes, he will have a bowel movement.

Additionally, you will certainly want to bring him outside any time that he makes a motion that implies that he needs to urinate or eliminate. This includes raising a leg or squatting, but also includes behavior such as pacing back and forth, pawing at the door or any other action that you may see as a possible sign.

The Signs

A very important part of successful housetraining is not only to bring a puppy to his bathroom area on schedule but also to keep a very close eye on him so that you will immediately notice if he makes a motion that implies that he needs to go out. This can only happen if you literally can see your puppy. If your puppy is allowed to roam the home without you, you will find urine and feces all over the house.

Remember that when someone says that a puppy has "had an accident" it technically is not an accident. What happened is that a bodily function occurred to the puppy while he was inside of the home because the puppy was not taken elsewhere in advance of that.

For the fastest road to success, you will want to be home with your puppy as often as possible. While you may work outside of the home or have other obligations that keep you away from home at times, any time that you can be home with your puppy, you should be. Once he is housetrained you will have your freedom back (at least to a much higher degree).

When you are indeed home, you will want to ensure that you keep your puppy close to you. The best method to do this, and to be able to walk around your home at the same time, is to tether your puppy to you. This will mean tying one end of the leash to you (your belt loop is suggested) and connecting the other end of it to your puppy. A "must" for any toy breed dog and highly recommended for any other sized puppy at all, is to use a harness as opposed to a dog collar. There is a very important reason for this.

All toy breeds and many small breeds are susceptible to collapsed trachea. Even medium and large breed dogs can suffer from this injury particularly when they are young puppies. Collapsed trachea is just as scary as it sounds.

The trachea (windpipe) is surrounded by rings of cartilage. Injury can cause a ring (or rings) to break and collapse inward. If this happens, it causes pain and breathing problems. It is a serious injury.

It can happen to any puppy if he is wearing just a dog collar and a leash is attached to it. If you are walking with your puppy, or if you have one end of the leash tethered to you so that you can keep an eye on him for housetraining purposes, the trachea can be injured if the leash to goes taut. Additionally, this can happen if the puppy jumps up or lunges forward...Or if you are walking, the puppy does not keep up and you accidentally drag him a bit.

While there *are* other causes for this condition, when an owner puts a harness on their puppy, it is a step well worth taking to help in preventing this sort of injury from happening. For all toy and small breed dogs, a harness is recommended at any time at all that a leash is connected to the puppy or dog.

For medium and large breeds, a harness is recommended during the puppy months.

For any sized dog of any age, a harness offers you better control over your dog and if you will be

training your dog to "heel", you may find a harness works wonderful.

The most important element regarding a harness is that pressure is not able to be accidentally put onto the puppy's fragile neck. With a harness, if the leash goes taut, the force will be distributed over the chest, back and shoulders, thus helping to avoid the possibility of collapsed trachea. Please do not wait until you see a puppy or dog with this injury, in pain and struggling to breathe, to understand the importance of this.

Some owners worry that a harness will be "too big" or "too heavy". The wonderful element about a harness is that most are actually very lightweight. There are many styles that do not weigh more than a collar. They are simply shaped differently so that a strap goes around the dog's chest and back.

Other owners worry that it will be "a hassle" to put a harness on. Yes, the first day that you use it, your puppy may put up a fight. However, just like every other element that your puppy will need to get used to such as sitting still for a bath, allowing you to clip his nails and tolerating a toothbrush when it is time for dental cleanings, your puppy will also get used to wearing his harness.

Harnesses are very popular at this time and you will find that they come in a variety of materials, sizes and colors. They can be a fashion statement as well as a method of having good control of your dog and all while protecting him from collapsed trachea.

With all of this in mind, it is best to have a harness on your puppy, with the handle end of the leash threaded up and over your belt loop and the other end attached to the harness.

At any time that you see that your female puppy is squatting or your male is squatting or raising a leg, slap your hands together loudly in order to startle him enough cause him to pause.

It is best if you lead him out to the designated area, however in some cases if your puppy cannot seem to wait, you may even need to carry him (and there may be a time or two that you find yourself running!). At this beginning stage, your goal will be to have as many "successes" as possible, even if it is to finish what was started indoors.

Helping a Puppy Develop His Muscles

As discussed earlier, a young puppy does not have full control over bowel and sphincter muscles. Keeping in mind that a 2 month old has only enough muscle control to hold in needs for 2 hours, if an owner continued to take a puppy outside every 2 hours as he grew older, he would not be able to fully work those muscles in order to *easily* hold on for 3 hours once he was 3 months old.

If an owner were to continue on in this way, bringing the puppy outside every 2 hours, even a 6 month old that would otherwise have learned control for up to 6 hours, would be "trained' by the owner to only hold on for 2 hours. *The dog would never be taught to hold his needs until his bladder was full.* The dog would naturally build up *some* muscles strength but usually not as much as he could have if otherwise helped along the way.

For this reason, each month as your puppy grows older, it will be important to wait a bit longer before bringing him outside. Certainly, if a puppy makes a motion to urinate or eliminate, he should be brought out. He should also be brought out each morning and each evening before sleep time. However during the day, try to stretch out the time in-between other outings. This allows your puppy to learn control over muscles that are fully capable of these gradual, incremental gains.

If you are home and 2 hours have passed and your goal is to make an increase to 2.5 or 3 hours, try to distract your puppy with some interactive play time. Even a grooming session may distract a puppy enough to forget about his needs and put those muscles to good use in holding his needs until the new longer time interval has passed.

Night Time Issues and Crating

One of the most frustrating times for a new puppy owner is being awakened at night by a barking or whining puppy. When awoken each night on a continual basis, sleep deprivation can quickly set in. This can cause an owner to feel more frustrated than he or she otherwise would...And before you know it, having that new puppy can seem to be very stressful. Luckily, there are answers to deal with this that will bring fast results.

The first element to discuss is crating. You may have heard that puppies and dogs will not urinate or eliminate when inside of a small enough crate. This is not true. They may resist doing so and they may try to hold on as long as possible. However, when enough time has passed that their muscles simply cannot hold in the urine or the bowel movement, they will indeed have no choice.

The bodily function will happen. It is not an "accident"....It is a natural, necessary and reasonably expected body function that  cannot be avoided no matter how much a puppy wishes to please his owner and no matter how much he does not desire to have urine or feces in his immediate area.

Therefore, a crate is not a "magical" method of "making" a puppy refrain from bathroom needs.

Staying too long in a crate and being forced to expel urine or feces in such a small area can cause quite a bit of stress to a dog of any age. Remaining in a crate with urine or feces is terribly uncomfortable and can cause anxiety. Consequently, keeping a dog in a crate for a long enough period of time that causes him to soil that very small confined area is akin to neglect.

There is a time and place for crates. Crates are fine to use for short bursts of time during the day in which you are unable to personally watch your puppy. They are also okay if used for a sleeping area, *only* when the dog is a puppy.

It is suggested to place a small baby blanket down in the crate so that your puppy is comfortable. If left to lie on a wired support for hours, this can cause sores and then ultimately possible loss of fur on those sore spots.

You may also opt to obtain a large enough crate so that a doggie bed fits inside. Once your puppy is trained to sleep through the night or to alert you to any bathroom needs, the bed can be moved out of the crate and the puppy will not need to become used to sleeping on a different surface.

"Bedtime" should be scheduled. Even if your own bedtime varies a bit, make sure that your puppy has a set bedtime routine. Food should not be fed one hour before bed, and this includes snacks. One hour before bed, all interactive play and all exercise should cease. 30 minutes before bedtime, lights should be dimmed and all sounds should be lowered such as the television. The goal will be to create a relaxing peaceful atmosphere that sends a clear message that the day is winding down and everyone is relaxing.

 Dogs are "crepuscular", which means that their natural period of peak activity is dawn and dusk. Ensuring that "bedtime" occurs at dusk, or 1 to 2 hours after dusk at the most, will allow a puppy to follow his natural body rhythm.

20 minutes before bedtime, a puppy should be quietly brought out to the designated area to see if he has to urinate or eliminate. Even if successful, there should be no playing afterward. Simply give praise and go back into the quiet, lowly-lit house.

At bedtime, gently place your puppy down, offer some calming words and gentle pats…And then leave. Your puppy will whine. Your puppy will probably bark. Unless 2 hours have passed do not respond.

During the night, if 2 hours have passed from when a puppy was "put to bed" or 2 hours have passed since he was last taken outside, an owner should respond to barking. Only about 50% of the time, the puppy will actually need to go. However, in order to find success with housetraining, this will need to be done for a limited temporary period of time.

The way that an owner reacts and handles things at night makes a *huge* difference in regard to success. A puppy must never be mistakenly "trained" that barking equals fun attention at night. If so, he may forever bark at night and intense training may be needed to reverse this.

It is much better to never reach that point. For this reason, if a puppy barks at night, no lights should be put on except for those absolutely necessary to see where you are going. There is no reason to stumble around in the dark… For safety reasons, it is suggested to use a flashlight to guide you.

An owner should not talk except for the key word of "Potty" if the puppy is indeed urinating or eliminating and "Good Potty" once the puppy has gone to the bathroom. The time spent outside in the middle of the night, patiently waiting for a puppy to find "just the right spot" should be spent in silence.

Owners sometimes find themselves talking out of habit, as part of them believes that saying "Come on, just go to the bathroom" will actually prompt a puppy to do so. This is not true. A puppy will perceive any communication of this sort to be interaction and attention. If done, a puppy may bark simply because he is lonely and will be mistakenly "trained" that barking at night equals his owner coming over, bringing him outside to walk around and paying attention to him.

If an owner is quiet and shows that barking equals a very short amount of time to go to the bathroom if necessary and *zero* playing, interaction or attention, in time a puppy will learn that barking at night is not very advantageous to him. Sleeping will appear to be the better option.

To summarize this particular topic, only respond to barking if the proper amount of time has gone by and when you do bring your puppy outside, do so with as little noise, light and talking as possible.

There will often be a period of 2 to 3 weeks in which a puppy will bark to high Heaven each night as if he was in terrible jeopardy, calling out for dear life, desperate for his owner to save him. If he has already gone to the bathroom and 2 hours have not passed by, do not fall for this misleading trickery.

While it is difficult to hear this barking, do remember that it is temporary. If you ignore it, you will allow positive changes to occur. As time goes by your puppy will be able to hold his needs for longer and longer periods of time. This will ultimately lead to your puppy sleeping through the night and there *will* be peace in the home. Keep this in mind, since usually even the direst of circumstances can be tolerated if a person knows for a fact that it is temporary. As long as you are following these guidelines, barking at night *will* be temporary.

When You Are Not Home

Housetraining can seem very daunting if you or any other person in your household cannot be home with a puppy; essentially leaving that puppy on his own. How is he to learn housetraining if no one is there?

The first element to keep in mind is that any time that you *are* home, strict housetraining policies should be followed without any lapses on your part. If no one will be home for a time period of more than the amount of hours that your puppy is able to hold his needs, a plan must be set up. Best would be a scenario in which you can have someone come to your home to bring your puppy out. This does not necessarily need to be a professional dog walker (which can be expensive).

If you have a family member, a neighbor, a friend or even know of a responsible teenager who would appreciate earning a few dollars for 15 minutes of "work" this can make it easier on your puppy. When taken out on schedule, the puppy will be able to stay with one training method.

If there is no other option but to leave the puppy home alone without a visit from someone, a little planning can help to make things easier. First, you will want to decide where you will have your puppy stay.

Crating a puppy all day is highly discouraged. A confined puppy will urinate and eliminate if he has nowhere else to go. Additionally, being confined to such a small area is a terrible way for a puppy to have to spend his day. Muscles cannot be stretched out, he cannot romp around...Boredom can set in easily and this creates destructive and sometimes hyperactive behavior when finally released.

It is best to choose an area of a room to gate off; the use of a baby gate often works well. Some owners prefer to designate a corner of a room (usually the kitchen) and use a gate to block off that area, allowing the puppy to have room to move, play, eat, sleep and importantly, go to the bathroom.

If your only option is to choose a corner of a carpeted room, it is suggested to obtain a piece of linoleum. This is rather inexpensive if purchased at a home improvement supply store. When placed down, it creates an area that can be easily cleaned up. You will simply be placing it down and not installing it, as it will be temporary.

Inside of the area should be a doggie bed (or soft baby blanket), toys (lots of them), water (in a dispenser so that it cannot be knocked over), food (if your puppy is still free-feeding or he will be home alone when it is meal time) and an area of pee-pads or newspaper.

Do keep in mind that in all likelihood, your puppy will chew up and move around the pads or newspaper. This is normal puppy behavior and can rarely be avoided. Also, it is a coin toss as to whether your puppy will actually urinate or eliminate on the pads or paper. However, being in a gated off section of the room, your puppy most likely will go to the bathroom away from his sleeping area, toys, food and water.

The negatives of leaving your puppy home alone is that any time that he goes to the bathroom when he is alone in his area, you miss out on an opportunity to teach a housetraining lesson and the puppy misses out on an opportunity to learn a lesson.

Being unavoidable in many situations, the upside to this is that the urine and feces are confined and if planned correctly, a puppy will usually only go to the bathroom one time while you are not home.

Roughly 30 minutes before you leave, go through each step in the housetraining process to offer the best chance of your puppy urinating, eliminating or doing both in his designated outdoor area before you leave. As soon as you arrive home, even if you see that the puppy has gone to the bathroom, do bring him outside for another try as it may have happened hours earlier.

When you are cleaning any mess that may have occurred, it is not worth the effort to complain or speak in a negative tone; your puppy will have no idea that you are referring to something that happened perhaps hours earlier. Your puppy deserves to be greeted in a very happy way as it is not his fault that he had to stay home alone with no access to his outdoor designated area.

As your puppy grows older, each month you will see marked differences in how long he can hold his bathroom needs. When all advice is followed that you have read throughout this chapter, his muscles will gain strength and soon you will be able to leave him home alone for the day with rarely an incident.

Indoor Training with Pee-Pads or Paper

Elements to Think About First

As discussed in the previous section, it is highly recommended to housetrain your puppy to go outdoors. While pee-pad training may seem like a great idea, owners often find it to not be so appealing after a while. For some, the idea *is* tempting at first. "Why not train my puppy to go to the bathroom indoors? It will just be like having a cat!" some will say.

This enthusiasm quickly fades away for many owners when they see how difficult it is for a dog to urinate or eliminate on such a small area as the dog struggles with not being able to choose "just the right spot", how the pad is often missed by just inches and the sometimes very overpowering smells and odors that build up over time.

Having pee-pads or papers down on the floor that a puppy (and then larger and older dog) uses as a bathroom can be compared to having a toilet seat in one of your main living areas, filled with urine and feces, not flushed for hours. An owner may build up a tolerance for the odor and often does not realize just how recognizable it is until a friend or neighbor embarrassingly brings up the subject.

Unless you live in a location that always receives snow or rain, going outside for bathroom needs is healthy for a dog, as it increases time spend outdoors in the sun and fresh air. While the bathroom process may only take ten minutes or so, being outside prompts many owners to then continue on with outdoor play or to then bring their dog for a walk, which is very beneficial to a dog's physical and emotional health.

Taking your dog for a walk is also very healthy for you! Dog owners are not just healthier due to companionship...Studies show that people who own *and* walk their dogs are 34% more likely to meet federal benchmarks regarding physical activity

than those who do not. And only about ½ of the population in America meet those benchmarks!

Keeping this in mind, you may still choose to housetrain indoors and if so, instructions follow in the next section. You will still want to follow all of the previous advice regarding times that a puppy will need to be brought to the designated area (the pads), how to help your puppy build muscle strength, noticing the signs, nighttime crating issues and advice for when you are not home.

Choosing an Area

The only difference, yet a huge one, will be that your puppy will be trained to urinate and eliminate in a designated indoor area as opposed to being brought outside. All other elements remain the same. All instructions regarding praise, when and when not to speak to your puppy, how to handle nighttime barking and all other elements remain in play.

Indoor training is more difficult than outdoor training; however an element that will greatly affect your level of success will be the area that you choose to place the pads down. *If* there will be times of having to leave your puppy home alone, the area for the pads should be the *same* area that you have set up for him for when you are not home. Therefore, in this case, there will only be *one* designated area. It will be one that he is confined to by gate when home alone and the same area that he can enter and exit at will when you are home.

If you will *not* be leaving your puppy home alone and have no need for a designated, gated off area, then you will need to choose an area for the pads. It is best to choose an area that the puppy can easily reach without a human having to open a door for him as you will want him to be able to walk over to that location any time that he wishes. You will not want it to be near any areas of foot traffic, in which people routinely walk by during the day or night.

Since a young puppy will often "miss the mark", if the area is carpeted it is suggested to place down a piece of linoleum. You will simply be placing it down and not installing it, as it will be temporary. As mentioned earlier, this is relatively inexpensive and can be purchased at home improvement supply stores.

Keys to Successful Indoor Housetraining

Following all of the previous advice, any time that your puppy shows signs or any time that a bathroom check is in order per schedule, you will bring your puppy over to the pads, repeating the key word of "Potty" or any other key word that you have chosen.

Even though you will be inside, do keep your puppy on a short leash. This will be needed to control his movements in order to keep him on the pads as you wait for him to urinate or eliminate. If you are using the tethering method to keep an eye on him, you will already have the leash attached. You may find it necessary to hold the leash in one hand and use your other hand to shorten it further, until the puppy's available space to walk is limited to being over the pad(s). Please follow all previous guidelines regarding a harness as opposed to a collar.

If your puppy seems to have trouble "hitting the mark", you can place down two pads, side by side. This offers him a larger area to target and will cut down on messes on your floor. As he learns his housetraining rules, you can overlap two pads to create a smaller area...and finally finish with placing down just one pad.

Remember that praise, words spoken or not spoken at night and all other elements must still be done in order to find success.

The "Puppy Pees"

It is normal for some puppies to urinate when excited. This is most common with puppies that simply become overwhelmed  with hugs, pats and kisses. The puppy will then have excitement urination behavior. Most will grow out of this phase. However, in the meantime, you may find a couple of things helpful.

 Try to play with your puppy outside as much as possible instead of indoors. Also, bring your puppy outside or to the pee pad to urinate before playtime, so that his bladder is empty before he becomes excited during play time.

If you have a puppy or dog that frequently becomes overexcited when you approach and urinates during this time (usually occurring if an owner has just returned home after being away for several hours), it is best to approach the dog from the side and slowly introduce play time.

Puppies, that display this behavior, should not be directly picked up. It is best to kneel beside your puppy, pat him a bit and then gently roll him onto your lap. This eliminates the sudden excitement of being picked up and hugged.

Housebreaking Set Backs

If your puppy was completely housetrained and then begins to urinate in the home, this may be caused by one of several issues.

A bladder or urinary tract infection - This is a serious health issue that can cause a dog to lose control of his bladder. Any time that a dog suddenly begins to have bladder control problems, a veterinarian checkup is necessary to rule out any medical issues.

If your dog is deemed 100% healthy, this may then be attributed to a behavioral issue.

If it has been determined that your puppy is healthy and this *is* a behavioral issue, it will be because of one of the following reasons:

Attention Seeking Behavior -   Even if owners are home with their dog, if they are busy and not paying attention to him, the dog may feel ignored and lonely.   When a dog urinates inside, suddenly he is seemingly receiving *tons* of attention!   People are dashing around, they are speaking to the dog… the house has come alive!

This does not mean that you must hug and play with your dog every moment...however, when you are home, try to take some time each hour to play, talk to or interact with him for about five or ten minutes. This will be in addition to the regular schedule that you keep each day, such as going for walks, grooming, etc.

Need for Approval - Even well trained dogs may sometimes need a reminder of just how great that they are doing. Positive reinforcement training should be used at this time. Although you probably did this when you were training your puppy, this may need to be done again, to remind your dog that urinating or eliminating in the designated area equals that he is being a good dog and that he receives praise from you.

Each time that your dog *does* urinate or eliminate in the appropriate place, behave as if he just did the most wonderful thing in the world. Talk with a very happy voice; say "Good Potty" and gives pats and hugs. Offer a small dog treat. Act very excited and happy. You do not need to do this forever, but only when your puppy needs a reminder.

Sending out your attention filled with praise when a puppy is behaving correctly works a million times better than reprimanding him for having accidents.

Older Dogs

When Bladder and Bowel Issues can Become a Concern

One of the signs of an aging dog is to lose some control of his bladder and/or bowels. As you watched your dog grow from a round little puppy into a mature, sleek adult your dog was loyal to you and loved you with all of his heart. Now a senior, your dog will need your understanding when he becomes old and has trouble controlling his urination and bowel movements.

No matter what the age of your dog, a medical checkup should be done to rule out bladder infection, bowel infections, urinary tract infection, tumors and more. If medical issues are not found, then your senior may have entered the phase of needing your help.

Doggie diapers work very well in this situation. Most dogs find them very comfortable and this allows an older dog to bypass the shame that a well-trained canine can feel when soiling inside of the home.

When an older dog that spent years
perfecting housebreaking, suddenly has
accidents, this can be stressful for him.

While there are some that disagree, many
studies show that canines feel many emotions
and embarrassment is indeed one of them. It
only takes a dog a week or so to become
accustomed to the doggie diapers.

House Training an Older/ Senior Dog

You may have gotten an adult dog for many
reasons and your adult may have come from
a breeder, rescue or other. In some cases, this
adult dog will already be house trained. In
other cases, the dog may need to be
reminded...or may need to learn from the
beginning.

If your adult is not house trained, ignore the
expression that "you can't teach old dogs
new tricks"...because of course you can!

Many adult dogs adopted from animal
shelters may not have gotten enough
opportunities to eliminate outside, and as a

result, they may have routinely soiled their kennel areas. This leads to a weakening of any previously learned housetraining habits.

Alternatively, scents and odors from other pets in the new home may stimulate some initial urination marking. Remember that you and your new adult dog need some time to pick up on each other's signals and routines. Even if your dog was housetrained in his previous home, if you don't recognize his "bathroom signal", you might miss his sign to go out, causing him to eliminate indoors.

Therefore, for the first few weeks after you bring your adult dog home, you should assume that your new dog isn't housetrained and start from scratch. If your dog was housetrained in his previous home, the re-training process should progress quickly. The process will be much smoother if you take steps to prevent accidents and remind your dog where he is supposed to eliminate.

If you clean up an accident in the house, leave the soiled rags or paper towels in the designated bathroom spot for a while if you are using the newspaper or "pee pad" method. The smell will help your dog recognize the area as the place where he is supposed to go.

While your dog is eliminating, use a key word such as "Potty,", that you can eventually use before your dog eliminates to remind him of what he is supposed to be doing. Feeding your dog on a set schedule will help make his bowels movements be more regular.

When You Are Not Able to Watch Your Older Dog

During the housetraining phase with an adult dog, there will be times when you cannot watch him at every moment. When you must go out to run errands, etc., your dog should be confined to an area small enough that he won't *want* to eliminate there, but *can* if need be.

The area should be large enough so that muscles do not cramp. Please do not crate an adult dog for longer than an hour. A gated off area, as previously described, works perfectly. Be sure to take your dog outside to urinate or eliminate right before you are to leave.

While it is rare for a senior dog to have the need for housetraining, if this is the case, do keep in mind that a senior dog may not be able to hold his needs for the 8 hours that an adult dog can.

Accidents

Adult dogs, especially senior dogs, will be prone to accidents. The older a dog becomes, you should expect this more. If you catch your dog in the act of eliminating in the house, do something to interrupt him like clapping loudly (don't scare him). Immediately take your dog to his designated bathroom area, give lots of praise, and give a treat if he finishes eliminating there.

Don't punish your dog for going to the bathroom in the house. The only goal will be to clean it up. Rubbing your dog's nose in it, taking him to the spot and scolding, or any other type of punishment will only make your dog afraid of you or afraid to eliminate in your presence. Dogs do not understand punishment after something happens, even if it's only a short time later. Reprimanding will do more harm than good.

Cleaning the soiled area is very important because dogs are highly prone to continue soiling in areas that smell like urine or feces.

Important "Accident Cleanup" Information

It is bound to happen when you have a puppy...And it does happen once in a while with "fully" housetrained dogs. Just when you least expect it or when it is the most inopportune time, your dog will have an accident in the home.

It is extremely important to clean the "accident spot" properly.... If any odor still remains, your dog will smell it, even if you do not...And that will lead him to being more prone to using that spot once again for his bathroom area.

If a Urine Spot is Still Wet

The best thing to do is to blot because blotting works much better than rubbing to lift urine up and out. Soak up as much as possible so that it does not begin to spread into the carpet backing or padding. Place a thick layer of paper towels (White only, so that the print does not transfer onto the carpeting) or an old towel on top of the area. Press or stand on the towels to help absorb as much of the liquid as possible.

Resist the Urge to Scrub if a Urination Accident is on a Carpet

Carpet fibers are twisted together and spirited rubbing causes them to separate. Instead of scrubbing, continue blotting until the area appears to be dry...then place some paper towels on the area, weighing them down with a book or a heavy object overnight to soak up any remaining liquid. If a stain remains once the area dries, try the steps ahead.

If there is no staining, your last step will be to remove any traces of odor. Remember that while you may not smell a thing, your dog likely does. Best is a high-quality pet odor neutralizer. This can be found at pet supply stores. Be sure to read and follow the directions for use, including testing the product on a small, hidden portion of carpeting first to be sure it doesn't discolor the fabric.

If a Spot Remains and is Dry

Dampen the area lightly with plain water using a sprayer bottle, a towel or a small handheld wet vacuum (if you have one). Avoid soaking the area, which can cause the stain to penetrate the carpet. You want to only mist the spot.

Using the small wet vacuum or paper towels, soak up the water, repeat the process of misting and extracting until the stain is no longer there. In most cases, plain water will work just fine.

Take it to the Next Level

If the spot remains, try a pet enzyme cleaner, found at pet supply stores or home improvement stores. Be careful not to reach for just any cleanser that you happen to have in your home. Many products such as disinfectants, solid surface cleaners, shampoos and powdered deodorizers can whiten a carpet or leave a residue that draws even more soil over time. Furthermore, avoid using ammonia or home-produced cleaners, which may get rid of the stench, but could soon afterward attract your dog to use that area again.

As mentioned previously, your last step will be to remove any traces of odor. Remember that while you may not smell a thing, your dog likely does. Best is a high-quality pet odor neutralizer. This can be found at pet supply stores. Be sure to read and follow the directions for use, including testing the product on a small, hidden portion of carpeting first to be sure it doesn't discolor the fabric.

Mysterious Odors

Have you ever caught a trace of a "dog" smell but you don't know where it is originating from? You can obtain a low-cost handheld black light (many are only about $20 at home improvement stores). When you sweep this over the carpet, the spot will light right up and you will know the exact spot to clean.

When Having an Accident is Not Just an Accident

While it is expected to have an occasional accident, if your otherwise well-trained dog urinates or has a bowel movement indoors, it *may* also indicate that he has a medical condition. You will want to make an appointment with the veterinarian immediately if:

 Your normally fully housebroken dog begins to have many accidents in the home. This could be from internal parasites, a bacterial or viral disease such as parvo (which can be fatal) or an infection.

 A bad odor is coming from your dog's mouth. If a canine's breath abruptly becomes unpleasant, it can indicate a more serious problem such as diabetes which often affects urination.

Marking Issues

A dog of any age may "mark" and this is not a housebreaking issue, it is a behavioral issue. Both male and female dogs mark. When a dog does this it is because he or she is marking their territory, not because they do not know where to eliminate or they do not understand the concept of housebreaking. Marking is not a method of emptying the bladder...it is a process of spraying out a bit of urine to mark territory.

This type of behavior is more common in multiple dog households. You will know that this is territorial marking behavior if a dog only urinates a little bit; as he or she will not release the entire contents of his/her bladder and will urinate only enough to mark the spot. The marking dog may keep urinating in the same spot or the same room.

Additionally, marking is the most likely explanation if the dog is housetrained and does not eliminate feces in the home, but only urinates inside. This is more common if a female is not spayed or if a male is not neutered. However, even if a dog is spayed or neutered, if there is another dog in the home who is not, this can cause this behavioral issue to develop.

These are the things that you can do to help prevent this behavior:

Clean the area, but not with a strong smelling cleaner. This can trigger your dog to try and mark yet again to cover that scent. You may wish to refer to the previous chapter of "Important "Accident Cleanup" Information"

If your dog has a near constant view of other dogs (for example, access to a window looking out into a neighborhood filled with dogs), try to limit his ability to see them. Just seeing another dog may trigger a dog to mark.

Try to turn the area that your dog is marking into a play area. Play with your dog there, give a treat, have him lie down and rub his tummy. If your dog begins to associate the area with play and fun, he will be less likely to mark it.

 If you have decided to spay or neuter all pets (cats too), now may be the time to do so. Dogs that are spayed or neutered are less likely to do this. Even if your dog is spayed or neutered, another pet that is not can trigger this behavior.

 As soon as you see that your dog gets into position to do this, make a loud noise to distract him (such as clapping your hands) and then immediately bring him to his designated bathroom area. Give great rewards if he urinates there.

Marking Behavior with More Than One Dog

In this case, a dog that is marking is most likely doing so because he or she feels the need to "make claim" of the house. Why? Because all dogs, of any dog breed, need to know the "order of the pack".

As touched upon earlier, long ago, dogs ran in packs and there was always a leader. Now, domesticated dogs still need to know: Who is in the pack? Who is the leader (the Alpha)? And a dog will question that if their human family member is the *top leader*, who is the leader *among the dogs*?

By following proper feeding methods, command training your dogs, grooming them, properly entering and exiting when taking them for walks and all of the care that you give, you have already shown them that in the pack, it is you who is the top leader. However, in a home with more than one pet, a dog that is marking needs to know who the leader in the sub-group of the animals is.

Usually, dogs will try to figure this out among themselves. However, doing so can be very stressful for all dogs involved. This can then lead to behavioral problems, such as this one. You can help by stepping in to establish which dog is the Alpha Dog.

It is typically the older dog. In some cases, it will be a strong female or the dog that lived in the home the longest. You can help determine which dog is exerting more desire for this role. Take notice when the dogs are playing. Is one of them more outgoing? Is one dog more "pushy" when it comes to choosing toys? Which dog runs and arrives at their food bowl first? Noticing this will help you figure out who is putting forth more effort to be the Alpha.

Once you know, you can then help both dogs. Remember that the dog that is not the Alpha dog is just as important and loved as the other dog. Not being the Alpha will make a dog be a Beta, still an important and integral part of the pack (household). Not being the Alpha dog is not a negative thing. Both dogs will be less stressed and happy, knowing their place in the "pack".

When it is time to feed dinner to your dogs, give the Alpha dog his food first. When it is time to take the dogs outside for a walk, put the leash or harness on the Alpha dog first. When you exit or enter the home the order should be: You, the Alpha dog and then the Beta dog. These small gestures help the dogs feel secure that you, the main leader, are showing them that you understand the "pack".

Heeling

Moving in Tandem

Heeling is almost like an art form. It is the rhythm of dog and human walking in unison. When heeling, while walking at the same pace, the dog is very aware that the human is in charge. The dog's human controls pace, direction and decides when to stop or reverse course. When your dog is fully  trained to heel, your dog will properly follow along whether you are walking, jogging or suddenly stop. A dog that heels always walks beside you and does not run ahead, lag behind or stop for any reason other than if you stop.

There will be plenty of times that you will not mind when your dog takes his time to explore the world. However heeling or not heeling can affect every day of your life; walking can be fun or it can be frustrating.

Some owners skip over this training because they believe that it will be too difficult. It is a shame since just one month of training can be the foundation for a lifetime of enjoyed walks. Another reason why owners do not train their dogs for this is that they expect their dog to naturally walk beside them. A dog has absolutely no idea that he is expected to walk nicely next to you.

Canine instinct does not tell a dog to walk beside a human, taking the owner's cues for speed and direction. This must be taught. When first brought out on a leash, a dog will do as he wishes. He will chase a butterfly, stop to smell flowers, try to run ahead and explore.

It is the owner who must show the dog what is expected. When a dog is trained in the correct way, learning to heel is not that difficult. Hopefully, you will be taking your dog for daily walks, which reinforces the learned behavior. A properly trained dog will always heel and walks can be fun without the stress (and sometimes embarrassment) of having your dog try to take *you* for a walk.

Heeling is when your dog walks on your left with his head no further ahead than the extension of your left heel. It is done this way because the majority of people are right handed. Having the leash in your left hand allows your dominant hand to be free. While this is the customary positioning, if you are left handed, feel free to train your dog to heel to your right if that is what feels best for you.

At What Age You Can Begin This Training

A puppy should be at least four months old before you begin any training outside of your home's property. Why? Because a puppy should not be brought to outside public places or to indoor public places until he has had all of his puppy shots. Once your puppy is up-to-date on all vaccinations, you may then go ahead and venture outside.

There is a short period of time in which the maternal antibodies that were passed from dam to puppy are too low to continue to provide the puppy with protection against disease, but too high to allow a vaccine to work. This phase lasts from several days to several weeks as it varies from puppy to puppy.

This time is called the window of susceptibility. During this "window", even though a puppy was vaccinated, he could still contract a disease. Because of this risk, any puppy that has not yet had his shots must be kept away from other animals or any places in which other animals could have previously been.

Once your puppy has had all of his puppy shots, you can then allow him to meet other people, go to parks, accompany you to stores, explore the world and importantly, learn to heel while out for daily walks.

If you have an older dog that has never learned to heel, it is never too late to train him. A dog of any age, other than perhaps a senior who is stuck in his own ways and has developed a lifetime of habits, will be able to learn to heel.

Training Your Dog to Heel – Step by Step Instructions

Before Heading Out

To begin, you will want to put a harness on your puppy. Walking an untrained puppy on a leash and *collar* can be very dangerous. As mentioned earlier, if your puppy lunges forward or if you pull too hard on the leash, the fragile trachea can collapse; this is a very serious injury. In addition, you will find that you have more control over your dog when training him to heel.

You will want to give your dog a few minutes to get used to the harness that you put onto him. Usually in just a matter of a couple of days, your puppy will accept it and not show any protest.

When exiting the home, you should exit first. After the walk is complete, you should enter back into the home first. This is part of training your dog to understand that you are the leader (the Alpha) and is discussed in detail ahead in a separate chapter.

Going for walks and having a dog learn to heel works best if walks are done at a certain time each day. Canines have amazing internal clocks, able to sense when things "should" happen. Dogs of all ages do best when they know what to expect. Be sure to choose a time that works for both of you. While you want to opt for a time that fits in well with your schedule and one that you feel comfortable with, also think about your dog's needs as well. You will not want to choose a time when he is normally tired and in need of a nap.

Just how do dogs know when it is time for dinner or time to go for a walk? Studies show that a canine's daily fluctuations of hormones, body temperature and

neural activity let them know wh
"should" happen.

Lastly, choose a special treat that you w give to your dog upon completion of the walk. The treat should be one that is not given normally as a snack. It should be special enough that your puppy learns that it is only given if a session of listening to you, such as this, occurs. Keep the treat hidden in a pocket so that your puppy does not see it or smell it, which would potentially cause him to pester you for the treat and not focus on the heeling lesson.

Heeling Rules and Guidelines

 Once you have chosen a good time for walks that works well for

you have him on a

n your pocket and

ne first with him

ow begin to walk.

: side.

...., ... y ... ..og ...es to walk ahead of you, stand in place and do not move. Using a harness, this will not injure or hurt your dog. Your dog may try several times to keep walking. Do not pull on the leash. Simply remain standing and do not move.

While you are remaining standing in one spot, essentially glued into place, any time that your dog comes very close to you, talk to him and pat him. This shows that staying near you means that the leash will not frustrate him.

As soon as your dog stops trying to walk ahead by himself and is remaining near you, give the leash a quick, light tug and continue walking. Hold the leash with two hands. With your dog on your left, you should be holding the leash tightly with your right hand and loosely with your left hand.

Anytime that your dog walks beside you, keep repeating the command word of "Heel" in a happy yet firm tone of voice so that he connects his actions with a command word.. Also, offer words of praise as you go along, first in the form of "Good Heel" to reinforce his actions and then with "Good Boy" or "Good Girl".

Change your pace; take turns walking slower and then faster. Do not just walk in a straight line; most dogs stay more focused if the walk is a fun challenge. You can help make this entertaining by winding around telephone poles, taking turns, and more.

You may need to tug and then say "Heel" over and over; however at any time that your dog is heeling, offer great words of praise. Do not stop to pat or hug your dog; but keep saying "Good Boy" or "Good Girl" and "Good Heel" in a very happy tone to show him how proud you are of him.

The first time that you take a turn and your dog does not, he will quickly realize that he must heel to you. You will make that turn and your dog (on harness and short leash) will have no choice but to follow along.

Of course, be very careful, as accidentally stepping on your dog can cause extreme injuries or worse. But, walk confidently and show your dog that you are in control. When this occurs, walk as if you do not notice that he is not exactly following along. The harness will not injure the neck and he will "catch up" to you as long as you do not increase speed.

These training sessions should be done each day, with each session lasting approximately twenty minutes. If you do not give up and you do this each and every day, your dog will learn what he must do to hear your happy "Good Boy" or "Good Girl" remarks.

When the walk is finished and you are still outside of your home, be sure to give your dog tons of pats, praise, attention and that tasty treat that you previously had put into your pocket. Remember that the treat should be a special one that is not normally given for snacks.

It usually takes about two weeks for a dog to really understand how to heel. Even when it seems that he is well trained, do keep offering the words of praise and the confirmation word of "Heel" as you walk along. Eventually, whenever you say the command word of "Heel" your dog will immediately go over to your left side and stay beside you.

Walking with Car Traffic

Some owners find that their puppy has trouble walking alongside traffic, even if they are safe upon a sidewalk. A puppy may shy away and be afraid to walk or he may bark excessively.

This will certainly happen if a dog is afraid of cars. We really can't blame them... puppies are so very little....think about how they feel when a big, metal car comes barreling down the street near them... They have no idea that a car (hopefully) will stay driving on the street. It would be like how a human would react if a cruise ship on wheels roared past us as we walked on the street.... Most of us would be very afraid and certainly on guard.

 If this is happening with your dog, the goal will be to slowly yet steadily teach him to not be afraid of cars. Do realize that the training for this takes time from your day but will be well worth it in the end. If not done, a dog may be afraid of traffic forever, or bark at cars forever. If done, the time taken out for this is temporary and the benefits are forever.

If you can spare about 20-30 minutes per day working on this, you should see good results within 2-3 weeks. When you begin training, you will want to stop taking him for his usual walk that involves walking where there are cars. To begin, you will want to take him for a walk on a very quiet street(s) where there are no cars. Having no cars, you can practice heeling without any of the distractions that are causing the issue.

If there are no areas of "zero traffic" near your home, you may find it helpful to drive to an area such as a business park (after hours) or a walking path.

After a few days of this, you will then want to find a route to walk on that has a few cars...not a lot... a street, perhaps in a quiet residential area that has 2-4 cars that would drive by slowly as you do a 20-30 minute walk. Before you leave for the walk, be sure to put some special dog treats into your pocket.

When a car inevitably passes by, do not tense up in anticipation. Continue walking. Your puppy may attempt to plant himself down firmly or try to lie down. This is one reason the harness comes in handy.

Keeping the same steady pace, continue walking, as if you are completely and utterly unaware that your puppy is attempting to either stay still or drop down. With the harness displacing pressure across the back, shoulders and chest (and not the neck as a collar would) you will cause no harm to him as long as you do not run.... Just walk at the normal pace that you established as your walk began.

If your puppy whines, talk in a matter-of-fact way as you continue on. Your goal is to 100% act as if you do not notice any change in your puppy's behavior. In leading by example, you will want to send the message that the car was no more important than a passing butterfly.

As the car passes and is gone from sight, your puppy is going to become confused for a moment.

The thoughts that pass momentarily through his mind are metaphorically going to be: "Oh my Gosh, that was terrifying, why in the world did my owner not notice that horribly scary thing!", "I am shocked that my leader continued to walk as if that frightening object did not exist... did my leader not notice that I was trying to blend in with the sidewalk?"....

"Wait a moment... things are starting to become a bit clearer...my leader, the person that I depend on for survival, was not afraid of that car at all, in fact he ignored it completely...Could it be?....Perhaps it is.... Yes, *perhaps* I was wrong to think that the car was scary"....

And now you are on your way to success. You have taught your puppy to rethink his reaction. You have taught your puppy to *consider* the fact that perhaps cars are not scary.

This is a turning point; but by no means will the training be done in one lesson. Now that you have taught your puppy to rethink his reaction, it is only by repeating this lesson will you then allow your puppy to not only rethink his reaction, but to strongly consider reacting in the opposite way.

By repeating further, you will then allow your puppy to not only consider reacting without fear, but to actually do so. When you repeat this lesson enough that your puppy handles a passing car without showing signs of fear, it is now time to give praise and reward.

Remember, earlier you were using all of your willpower to ignore him; therefore rewards did not come into play. Now, you are at the point that good behavior receives both praise and reward.

After one week of handling a certain intensity of traffic in a calm manner, you can then take things up one level, choosing a walking route that is a bit busier. Handle each passing car as described earlier...ignoring the negative behavior and marking good behavior with reward.

Resistance to Walking

Some dogs are very resistant to walking and in many cases this can be contributed to the surface that they are being asked to walk upon. When a person is wearing shoes, it is very easy to forget that street surfaces can be extremely hot if the weather is warm and sunny. While a dog's paws are sturdy, they are made of skin, albeit thick skin. They have nerves that feel burning sensations, pain and/or injury.

What is the texture and temperature of the surface that you are walking on? Forget that you have shoes on and look at it from your dog's point of view. Are there lots of pebbles or rocks? Is it hot or cold when you touch it with your hand? If so, doggie shoes can be implemented. Alternatively, if heat is the reason for resistance, you may opt to walk in the early morning or late afternoon when surfaces have cooled down.

Also, check the weather in regard to how your dog may physically feel when exercising outdoors. If it is very warm to hot, bring lots of water and take rests in the shade if at all possible. Is it cold? Putting a sweater on your dog may be all that is needed to keep away a chill and allow for important exercise.

In addition, your dog may not want to go for walks when you do. Try to learn what time of the day your dog *wishes* to have exercise. Most will have pent up energy at a certain time of the day and it is then that they would *love* to release it. Every few days, choose a different time to see if the enthusiasm level of your dog is higher.

Just as some humans like to exercise in the morning, others like to take walks at lunch time and yet others prefer evening workouts... so may your dog. Working together, you should be able to pinpoint the time in the day that your dog most wishes to stretch his legs and accompany you for a journey around the neighborhood. Once he has learned to heel, you can then adjust the time of the daily walk to better fit your needs and schedule, if this is desired.

Some dogs are very sensitive to ground texture and sand can be a big factor. It is so much fun to walk along the shore of the ocean, a lake or another body of water that has a sandy shoreline...But the sand particles can cause a puppy to feel discomfort and this should be looked at if your puppy is resistant to walking on this type of surface.

Sand particles are very tiny. When walking on sand, it is quite possible that some particles can become stuck between paw pads or that the particles are very irritating to his paws (and the sensitive skin between the pads).

If your dog is walking along the sand and suddenly shows signs of discomfort, stop to inspect all four paws. Look for any bits of particles...or any redness, swelling or any sign of irritation. If there *are* particles stuck into the paw, it is best to rinse them off in the bathtub or kitchen sink and flush the paw...Then pour a bit of hydrogen peroxide on the area. Later that day, or the next day, you can apply some paw wax onto the pads.

If there are not any sand particles, but there is any redness, swelling or other signs of irritation, it will be best to bring your dog to the veterinarian. A cut may have gotten infected and an antibiotic medication and/or topical treatment may be needed.

If it is simply a matter of a dog resisting a walk upon sand yet it is not causing any injury, it will help to protect the paws with shoes or doggie booties if you wish to continue to routinely walk there. Trying to force a dog to walk upon these types of textures will not bring success...Your choice will be to either avoid the area or put foot protection on your dog to bring about results that can lead to a relaxing walk along the shore.

If using doggie booties or shoes, it is suggested to first have your dog wear them at home before going out for a walk with them on. When you put them on, cuddle your dog into your lap and slip them on while talking to your dog in order to distract him. For that very first time, leave them on for about an hour and see how he does. The next day, have him wear them for perhaps for two hours. When your dog seems to forget that they are on him, this is a good time to head out for a walk.

Some dogs need a bit of encouragement to join their owner for a walk. The tone your voice will send a message as to whether your dog should perceive a walk as a fun activity or a dreaded undertaking. Dogs pick up on not just the words that we say, but also in the way that we say them.

When getting ready to leave for a walk, it will be helpful to sound very excited. Talk as if you are about to leave on an amazing journey. Act enthusiastic. And do use a very loving but firm voice... It may take a couple of days like this to send the message, but it should lead to a dog thinking the equivalent of, "If my human is excited about walking, maybe I should be also!"

If a dog truly shows a strong dislike for walking and basically plants his paws down, ready to hold his ground, refusing to move, treats may be needed to use as motivation. If this is the case, when you are out, any time that your dog is walking nicely with you, randomly give him treats. It is suggested to offer truly exceptional treats if a dog needs a lot of incentive.

One treat that works very well in this situation is crisp bacon. Bacon is actually not an unhealthy food if it is given in moderation and prepared properly. It is suggested to fry it or microwave it to a very crisp texture. Doing so releases much of the fat. Then, you will want to put the pieces between paper towels and squeeze it all together, so that the paper towels soak up most of the remaining fat. What you are left with are crisp pieces that are 95% meat.

As a last step, crumble the bacon up, so that you have small little pieces. You can put them into a plastic sandwich bag and have that bag in your pocket. Then, as you are walking...every now and then repeat the word "Heel", walk for a few more seconds, say in a happy tone "Good Heel!" and then without pausing much at all, reach into your pocket, grab a pinch of the crumbled up crisp bacon, and put it right in front of your dog's mouth so that he can quickly eat it.

Details of How to Have a Well-Mannered Dog

The Type of Relationship that You Have

Through the Eyes of a Dog

To have a well-mannered dog, it all comes down to how your dog sees you. Does he see you as an equal? Does he see you as someone that he can manipulate? Or does he see you as a loving and kind leader? Only when a dog sees his owner as a loving and kind leader, will that dog *be able* to be well-mannered. Dogs that do not see their human as the leader will have internal struggles that prevent them from listening, obeying and behaving...even if they wanted to, canine instinct prohibits it.

As discussed earlier, in the mind of a canine, he is living in a pack. The pack consists of all humans and any other animals that are living together in the household. The members of each pack (household) holds a rank. The highest rank is Alpha. This means that the person (or animal) who is an Alpha is recognized as being a leader. All humans should be seen as Alphas. Under the rank of Alpha will be Beta. Those who follow the rules that the Alpha sets into place are Betas. Betas are important members of the family. Being a Beta does not reduce the amount of love shown or decrease the amount of care given.

Trouble can set in if a dog assumes that he is an Alpha. A dog may assume this if he is not taught otherwise, as a dog may believe this to be true if an owner does not clearly teach him the proper ranking.

When a dog sees himself as being an Alpha, he will basically do as he pleases. A dog will then display behavior that includes barking, nipping, chewing, begging for food, running around silly, not heeling when walking, being resistant to following commands and essentially being a huge deciding factor in the peace level of a household.

Dogs that do not see their human as the Alpha, will behave in a way that is dictated by canine instinct. Seeing their human as a Beta, canine instinct tells them that they are *not* to listen to a Beta. *For these dogs, they are essentially being taught to not listen.* To have a well-mannered dog, an owner must usually teach their dog to accept the fact that the human is the Alpha and the dog is the Beta: important, loved and cared for yet ultimately fully expected to listen to the human Alpha.

If an owner has not established himself as the clear leader, a dog may or may not listen...generally a dog will then only follow a "command" if he is good and ready to do so. This can give an owner a false sense that a dog listens...however, it will be a case of a dog really only following what seems to be a good idea to him at the time.

This is why an owner may wonder, "Why does my dog listen to me when I call him to go out for a walk, but ignores me when I command for him to sit?" In this case, the dog came when called because the dog wanted to go for a walk. He did not sit on command because he did not want to. *He was never following any commands in the first place.*

However, when the "leader" requests something, a dog will obey. When an owner establishes himself as leader it not only *allows* a dog to listen and follow commands, that owner is also allowing their dog to be happier. With the question of "Alpha" settled, a dog feels secure. He knows that his needs will be met. He knows that he is safe and that his pack is secure and running well.

And importantly, he will not need to endure the stress that occurs when a dog is not sure if he is Alpha or Beta....and he struggles to find out. How will he try to find out? By testing you...He will misbehave and see if you intervene in the way that a true Alpha would.

Dogs that are Betas are much better behaved. And studies have shown that they are smarter as well since they are more capable of taking in and retaining information including commands and understanding words that are spoken in every day conversations.

Your Dog's Happiness

Let's talk about your dog's happiness for a bit... When a puppy or dog has the secure feeling that his human is the leader, he can relax. All dogs have a strong instinct to know *exactly* where their place is in the pack (family). When this is not clear to them, an internal struggle begins...They become confused and they do not know whether they should listen to orders...and will often be reluctant to do so as their mind ponders whether they should step down and listen or purposely not listen to hold or gain authority.

A physical struggle begins as well. A dog that is unsure of his place, not knowing if he must take charge or if his owner should, will begin to test this. He may growl when being groomed...he may not come when called, a dog may chew on your favorite shoe...the list is endless. He will do these things to test your reaction and to see if your actions and words show that he is the leader *or* if your actions and words show him that he needs to listen to you.

Dogs *want* to have a leader. They are so much happier when they can relax knowing that you will provide food, shelter, and all of the things that make their life nice. The world is a big place, even your neighborhood seems enormous to your dog. He will be much more relaxed and happy when he does not need to worry about anything and decisions are left in your capable hands.

Dogs are content when they know what to expect. They like to know for certain that good behavior equals attention and treats. They feel that "all is right" when they receive praise for listening. When they know that the owner is the Alpha and they are the Beta, they are then able to see the world in black and white (a ranking that makes sense to them) and not in shades of gray where they are having internal resistance and struggles as they try to figure it all out.

How This Affects Learning

When your dog sees you as the Alpha, and any internal struggles that he had in regard to trying to figure out ranking are done with, he is then able to concentrate on command training. This means that with consistent

training, your dog will steadily learn the meaning of the words that you say.

He will be much more willing to practice with you. He will have more enthusiasm to go through the learning steps. This leads to a well-trained dog. And a well-trained dog is a confident dog. That is a wonderful gift that you can give to him.

When a canine is taught something, the act of doing so develops brain cells. It builds stronger and faster cerebral connections. This then leads to further success in learning new commands, tricks, and more. And this all leads to a more intelligent dog. A Beta dog will have the ability to respond quickly to commands, he will have the ability to comprehend words, and he will have the ability to more swiftly learn any new commands that an owner wishes to teach.

Establishing Your Role

This is best done when a dog is a puppy, nevertheless any dog of any age can be trained...Therefore an older dog that has been reigning over the house can be shown that it is time for a new Alpha.

There are some things that should always be done a certain way. Many owners do these things without giving them a second thought. When doing these things in a specific way, these little elements all come together to teach your dog that you are the loving and kind leader.

Feeding Your Dog

Feeding your dog is a huge element in establishing yourself as Alpha. Some owners do not think about this and simply place their dog's food bowl onto the floor. If it is not done correctly, the owner then walks away and is completely unaware of the strong statement that has just been made and the detrimental lesson that their dog just learned.

To a dog, food is survival. Even for the most spoiled pets that are given the world, canine   instinct dictates that it is food that equals their very existence. If food is placed down without much thought, even if that meal is one worthy of a royal pet, a dog will not have a clear understanding of where the food came from. A dog will think that the bowl "magically" is now filled with tasty food and will eat it without rationale as to how the food arrived there.

When feeding your dog, it is a tremendous opportunity to teach him that you are the Alpha. If a dog learns that his human only gives him food after careful consideration and that the action of placing down the food is a deliberate and clear decision by his owner, he then sees that human as his leader.

While not always possible, it is best if at least one of your dog's meals is given when you are also eating a meal. This is the strongest way to teach the Alpha/Beta lesson. When doing this training, you will want to prepare your meal (or the whole human family's meal) and also your dog's meal at the same time. Place your dog's bowl up on top of a counter so that he cannot reach it.

Then, sit at the dinner table and make sure that your dog sees that you have begun eating first. If he sees his food and jumps up at it, begs for it or begs for some of your food be sure to 100% utterly and completely ignore him.

After he sees that you have started eating, only then should he be fed. You do not need to make him wait very long; all that is needed is to for your dog to see that you are eating for as little as 30 seconds. Then, it will be time to place his bowl down in the proper way.

Before you offer him his food, first he must show that he agrees that you are Alpha by sitting on command in his designated eating area. This will also halt any jumping/begging behavior that began when he saw that you were eating first. Ahead, you will be able to read detailed instructions regarding training your dog to sit.

Once he is in the "Sit" position, you can place down the bowl, release him from the sit and allow him to begin eating. Once he begins, you should then continue on with your meal. This was a fast lesson but *oh-so important* in establishing your Alpha position. This feeding method should be done for life; it will be done when teaching the Alpha/Beta lesson and then done from that point on to reinforce this.

The Doorway

The simple action of entering and exiting the house is often done without pause. Most owners do not think about this yet most dogs see this as an important statement. To a dog, the order in which all household members enter and exit the home is a clear signal of who is Alpha and who is Beta. This will include all humans and all pets.

The order that all members of the household should enter and exit is: Humans and then dogs. If you have more than one dog, while you want to establish that you are the Alpha of the home, within the subset of animals, one dog will be the Alpha dog and the other(s) will be the Beta dog(s). Usually dogs figure this out on their own and most often it will be the older dog that is seen as the Alpha dog.

Therefore, in a multiple dog household, the order will be: You, any other humans, the Alpha dog, and then the Beta dog(s).

Never allow your dog to run outside ahead of you. To help with this, an owner should always put their dog on leash to control the order of the entering and exiting. If a dog normally is let outside to an enclosed area, such as a fenced in backyard, it is best if the owner exits first followed by the dog. Once outside, the owner can then go back inside if the objective was to have the dog spend some time in the yard, unsupervised but in an enclosed, safe area.

You should exit and enter first no matter what the reason is for leaving the house, whether it is to bring your dog outside for bathroom needs or to go out for the daily walk.

If a Dog is Very Stubborn

There are some dogs that will need a message that is clearer and more to the point. For very stubborn dogs, an owner will need to send a message that cannot be misunderstood. It will be a message that is so strong that no dog will challenge it.

Please note that this does not involve hurting your dog in any way. This must be done exactly as described so that your dog is not accidentally injured. The purpose of this is to show him that you are the leader while still being loving and kind; no mistreatment is involved. It should be done without scaring him. It should be done with love....after all; your goal is a happy, well behaved dog.

If your puppy growls at you or shows any strong signs of challenging you for leadership, you should do the following as it will send an undeniable statement that you are the Alpha:

 Turn your puppy onto his back with his tummy facing up toward you.

 Spread out your fingers and only with enough firmness so that he cannot wiggle free, place your hand across his tummy.

Your thumb and pinky should be near each armpit of the puppy and the rest of your hand gently across the tummy, with only enough pressure that he *can* wiggle but *cannot* wiggle free.

 Now, you wait. He will struggle, squirm and make just about every moment that you can imagine in order to break free.

 Finally, he will give up. He will be looking up at you with those puppy dog eyes and he will calmly lie still under your loving hand. This means that he has submitted to you...which is equivalent to him saying, "Okay, you win, YOU are the leader".

Important

An owner should *never* ever hit, yell or try to instill fear into a dog to make him obey. A dog will not respect an owner who does that...He will fear him! And that is not the relationship that one wants. The relationship between dog and owner should be one of true love and caring.

Remember, a dog that follows your commands and sees you as the authority figure is a happy dog and a well behaved dog. He will still be silly, he will be amusing, he will not be afraid of you...he will be relaxed. And he will soak up and love the praise that you give to him when he listens to you.

Command Training

What Your Job Will Be

The Objective

As discussed earlier, command training brings so many benefits to both owner and dog. The most obvious benefit will be that your dog will listen to you. Your puppy will learn to sit and stay as soon as you give the commands. Just these two commands alone can make a world of difference.

When an owner properly teaches commands, it does much more than teach a dog to perform certain actions. As a dog is learning the meaning of a particular command, that dog is also learning that the owner is the leader (the Alpha). This creates a relationship between owner and dog in which the dog is ruled by instinct to listen to the leader. A trained dog will behave better in all aspects and will be a pleasure to have as a companion.

Obedience training is the hallmark of a well-behaved, well-mannered dog. A dog that sits, stays and comes to you on command is showing refined behavior and displaying gracious intelligence.

A puppy can begin learning tricks as young as 8 weeks old. If you do have a puppy, it is best to perhaps work in one command at a time... as you will have your hands full in teaching your dog about housetraining, sitting nice for grooming and more. And older dogs *can* certainly learn new tricks. Older dogs can still have sharp minds and while they may not want to play as much as when they were puppies, many still enjoy learning new skills.

Your Part

Your job as a trainer is to direct your dog in a consistent and encouraging way. Your goal will be to guide your dog through the progression of executing a new skill or behavior, rewarding incremental progress along the way.

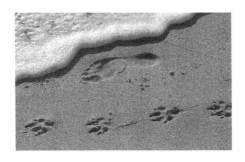

It is very important to understand that when you are teaching your dog to follow a command, this is not achieved in one day. It is a step-by-step process....and little by little, with your help, your dog will learn to master the particular commands. The goal of each training session will be to attain better results than the earlier session... If that happens, things are going in the right direction.

Consistency

Understand and recognize the exact behavior that you are looking for and do not be indecisive about this... Use the same voice and inflection each time that you give a verbal command to your dog ...and articulate the words very clearly.

Motivation

You will want to understand that during training time, you are your dog's coach. Part of the responsibilities for this job is to offer motivation. As a coach, you will want to be optimistic even if your dog becomes discouraged. It is at that time that he will need to hear you say "Good job!" if he is trying.

The level of enthusiasm that you put into your dog's training will affect the speed of his learning. And when your dog does something correctly, be sure to use a high-pitched, happy tone of voice to show him your delight. Your reactions to his actions will hold a great deal of weight.

Hesitation

Imagine that you are at work alongside a co-worker and friend. Now imagine that you did something well and were looking for a praising comment but your co-worker ignored you and you heard none. Then, thirty minutes later out of the blue, your co-worker suddenly yelled, "Good job!"

If this happened, you would be confused about his or her comment. You would not make an immediate connection of your co-worker's seemingly out of the blue remark to the task that you completed a half hour earlier. This scenario can be applied with dog training and is an illustration of how important it is for a dog to receive praise as soon as he performs.

Canines perceive time different than humans and they make connections between actions and words quickly. If there is hesitation, a dog can become confused. If a dog follows a command, but is praised and rewarded even five seconds afterward, he can think that he is receiving praise and reward for whatever it is that he is doing at that very moment and not for what he did earlier.

For example, if a dog sits upon command but then rises, and an owner hesitates, thereby giving a "Good Sit!" confirmation once the dog has stood up, the dog will think that the reward was given for standing and not for sitting.

When training, it is imperative that an owner mark the *exact* moment that the dog performed correctly. Marking this exact moment will be done by the owner giving praise (if the dog gave a good effort) or a treat (if the dog accomplished the desired action).

Motivators/Rewards

Dogs, in general, want to please their owners...And while pleasing a human is *part* of what will motivate a dog, envisioning a reward creates more enthusiasm. A motivator, or reward, for performing a skill can come in different forms... a special treat or a toy. As we move through the process of command training, most instructions will be to give your dog a treat.

Most dogs are food motivated...Treats are quick to dispense and be swallowed...and are a fast method of signaling a dog's correct response.

In the beginning stages, you will want to keep motivation very high by having the treat be something very special. A snack that would normally be given will not have a lot of meaning.

There are several "special" treats that you may wish to choose from for command training. Some dogs love sweet snacks and for those, apple pieces work great. Be sure to never give your dog a full apple, as the seeds are toxic. Cutting up an apple into pieces, putting the slices into a plastic sandwich bag and then giving those out for reward works very well.

For dogs that are "meat motivated", bacon that is cooked very well (crispy) with the majority of the grease being dabbed up with paper towels works well; the bacon can then be crumbled into small pieces. Alternatives are turkey meatballs, turkey hotdogs (cut into little pieces) or a high quality manufactured dog treat (best is organic without artificial coloring).

A Change in Motivators

You will not need to forever offer treats to mark the moment that your dog obeys your commands. As you progress in training, your dog will gradually follow along out of habit. This means that he will eventually follow commands on cue, without a second thought. Humans have automated responses all of the time and canines can as well.

If you command your dog to sit one hundred times and he sits those one hundred times, it then becomes an instinctive action. For the first one hundred times, a dog may sit because he was motivated to do so by the temptation of a treat. However, later, his muscle memory responds to the command of "Sit" and his body moves into a sitting position.

It is at this point that an owner can start to use less and less treats, treating every other time and then only randomly. After training is complete, a dog should be given treats as rewards once in a while to reinforce good behavior so that he will never forget commands or think that listening is negotiable.

"Must Haves" for Helping Your Dog Be Successful

A Lot of "Good Dog!" Remarks

A huge factor in regard to keeping a dog motivated is to keep him challenged, and feeling that he regularly achieves success. It is best to not allow your dog be wrong more than three times in a row. If he is "wrong" more than three times, he can quickly become discouraged and not wish to continue practicing.

Therefore, if you see that your dog is struggling and cannot fully achieve a skill after three tries, go back to an earlier step in the training. When you do this, your dog will be able to receive praise for what he *is* able to accomplish.

After a couple of more sessions at this lower level, you can then see how he does when taking it up a notch. Chances are that the additional positive reinforcement is what will push him over the hurdle and allow him to continue on with the next steps.

Time

When teaching a dog a new command, it can seem as if your dog is not getting the hang of it and has no idea what the command is supposed to mean. A dog may wiggle, try to play with you or only focus on the treat that he knows is in your hand. Do not become discouraged as this is normal for many dogs and you still *can* be successful in training.

Remember that there is no rush and your dog does not need to be fully trained by any particular date. With this in mind, try to have a relaxed attitude but do be sure to practice each and every day.

In the event that you simply must miss out on a day of training, this will not affect your overall success.   While it is not ideal, one missed day will not be the deciding factor as to whether or not your dog can be trained.

What Can Cause a Roadblock

A very common reason for a dog not learning commands is directly related to a low level of an owner's patience.   Just as with housetraining, an owner cannot expect things to be done in one day or even one week. Training should not be done unless it can be done in the spirit of having fun, if an owner has time to not rush to find success within just a few days, and if the owner can be in a good, positive mood while training.

Progress happens, even if you do not see it. Small steps are taken each time you have a session.

For example, even if your dog does not fully sit during an entire session of "Sit" command training, he will be hearing the word of "Sit" and he will therefore be learning that it means *something*....even if it takes him a few more sessions to understand what it is that it means. His mind is at work, even if his body is not showing it. If you do not give up, you will soon see that it was all worth it as you will have a well-trained dog for life.

Moving Your Dog into Position

It may be tempting to manipulate and move your dog's body into a desired position such as "Sit" because it is brings fast results; however those results are extremely temporary and do not allow a dog to learn. It is a shortcut that will not bring true success. While you may need to slightly manipulate him into certain positions, this must go hand-in-hand with enticing him with a treat and providing encouragement.

When you move a dog to "Sit", this carries the message that it is your idea and yours alone. When you *entice* a dog to "Sit", he starts to think that it is his idea and *that* is what brings victory. You will be enticing him to follow a command; it will be *his* decision to actually do so.

The Word You Should Never Say

To be successful, you will never want your dog to feel as if he is doing something wrong and thereby causing your displeasure. If this type of atmosphere is created, a dog may then have no interest in training due to anxiety that is produced when being "wrong" too often.

Therefore, when you are training, never use the word "No" as it can give a dog great pause. If your dog is not following along, remember that learning a command takes time and a dog needs a lot of repetition to fully understand it. "Practice" is another word for "training". Therefore, keep this in mind. Training your dog means that he will be practicing and this will take place over the course of a couple of weeks with increasing levels of success reached along the way.

Keep up morale and create an environment of enthusiastic learning. If your dog does not sit, stay or follow any other command exactly was you wish, say, "Uh-oh!" instead of saying "No".

The Release Word

Your dog will need to understand at which times he is under your control and at which times he has been released from the command. When instructed to "Sit" or to "Stay", your dog will be expected to remain in those positions until you "release" him with a chosen release word. After all, "Sit" does not carry much weight if your dog only sits for a split second!

When training canines, the most widely used release word is "Okay", and this works well for the majority dogs. One reason why it works well is that most dogs only pay attention to the first syllable of a word or to the strongest sounding syllable. Canines can become confused if two words sound similar. The word "Okay" is short, very distinct and a dog will not confuse this with any other words normally said to him.

Training should be thought o   ...g process. There will be the time that you teach your dog and then from that point on those lessons should be reinforced. Once it appears that a dog has learned a command, an owner should give that command at least two times per day when at all possible. If not, a dog can quickly forget all of the hard work that it took to reach that level of success.

While you may at first think that it will be difficult to remember to give the commands each day, you will find that most are given naturally. For example, "Sit" will be given before your dog eats and you may find yourself giving the command to him when you wish to put him on leash or you are preparing to brush out his coat.

"Down" is often given if a dog is acting too hyper or if he doesn't seem to understand that it is time for bed. "Come" will be used quite a bit and is almost always said when you want your dog to trot over to you to be readied to go outside for a walk.

One command that may not usually be said as a normal part of your day will be "Stay". However, this command is very important and on the occasions that you do need to use it, you will be very happy that you took the time to teach it and that you took the time to reinforce it.

It can be helpful to try and get into a habit of using it before a task that you know that you will be doing nearly every day. An example would be if you fall into the habit of commanding "Stay" after you enter the home when returning from a walk with your dog. He can be commanded to "Stay" while you take off your shoes or do another fast task that would come naturally to you.

Another important command that may not be automatically said each day is "Give" or "Give it to me please". As with "Stay" you can incorporate this into your daily routine. Once a dog has learned "Give" or "Give it to me please" an owner can teach his or her dog to pick up a ball and pass it over before regular games of catch...Or an owner can make things fun by allowing the dog to be part of a chore.

One example is when clothes are being folded...once a dog understands the "Give" command, he can be taught to mouth a clothing article and hand it over to the owner. This can be done over and over, allowing a dog to be very happy to help out while prompting the amusement of his owner and it can make household chores fun.

The Top Tens

Before you begin with command training, let's go over the top 10 elements to remember as you begin this fun journey.

 Reward with special treats, not ones that your dog would receive throughout the day as a regular snack.

 Reward at the exact moment that your dog is in the correct position or has just done the command that you asked for.

Don't waste precious time by rummaging for the treat. Have one in your hand, ready to give to your dog immediately.

 It is best to train when your dog is hungry. Therefore, right after dinner is not a good time.

 Training should be done before playtime. Once the session is done, you can then allow your dog to run around and play or you can engage him in a game.

 Always end each session when your dog is doing well. Even if you must go back to an earlier level in the training, do so in order for your dog to hear praise. In this way, he will be much more eager to practice again the following day.

 Be consistent. If you decide to train your dog, be sure that you can devote at least 20 minutes each day, divided into two 10 minute sessions. Always be consistent with the words that you say and be consistent with how you follow the steps for each command.

 Have true enthusiasm. Dogs pick up on our non-verbal cues as well as the tone of our voice. If an owner says, "It's a great day, I feel wonderful." but this is said with a sad voice and the person slumps down in a chair while saying it, a dog will know that their owner is implying, "This is *not* a good day."

Train your puppy or dog when you are in the mood to do so and this will lead to you feeling good about it and thereby passing that feeling down to him. Your dog will pick up on your tone of voice and body language to determine if you are actually excited about the training.

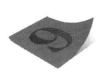 Be patient. Training for "Sit" takes an average of two weeks, if an owner practices with a puppy two times a day, every day. Other commands may take longer. Usually, with consistency, no command will take more than four weeks. Never compare your puppy's learning rate to

that of any other dog. A dog will learn one command quickly and will need to work longer on another.

 Instill the knowledge. Once it appears that your dog has learned a command, he will soon forget it if you do not use that command on a regular basis. For each basic command such as "Sit" and "Stay", you will want to use each, at least two times per day.

A dog is not fully trained until he follows a command each and every time it is given, without hesitation. If commands are not reinforced, a dog can forget them in as little as one or two weeks.

The Wording and Instructions

You will find that with the following command training instructions, the guidelines may be slightly different than what you may have previously heard, read about elsewhere or have done in the past.

For example, when you read about which words to use to show your pleasure that your dog performed well, it is important to say the *exact* wording.... Saying "Good Dog" is the most *common* response that owners give, but it is *not* the best one. The fastest road to success is to reinforce the dog's comprehension of the command while praising. Therefore, for example, a happy and enthusiastic, "Good Sit!" will be given upon a successful sit and not just "Good Girl" or "Good Boy".

The "Sit" Command

"Sit" as well as "Stay" and "Come" are commands that are the foundation of a life time of learning ....Learning more words, learning more tricks, learning more commands. It also is part of the foundation for good behavior and having a well-mannered dog. These three commands are often referred to as "simple" or "basic" commands, yet this terminology can be misleading.

While they may seem to be "simple" to some (mostly be those who are not dog owners), many owners find frustration with the training for one or more of these commands. Why? Well, there are some very common mistakes that can be easily be made that will severely impede a dog's learning process.

As you go through these commands, it will be important to follow them exactly for the fastest road to success. Additionally, while it is possible to train a dog for two different basic commands at the same time (done during separate training sessions over the course of each day), it is recommended to train "Sit" before "Stay" and "Stay" before "Come".

As we progress into more complicated commands and even some tricks, a dog will need these "foundation" commands in order to learn other, more challenging ones.

The Goal

The goal of this command will be that when the command "Sit" is given, your dog will sit squarely and firmly down on his hindquarters and remain in that position until you give the "release" word.

What You Should Know About this Command

Puppies as young as seven weeks old can start learning this command and it is often the first command that a dog is taught. This command is the foundation for essentially all other commands. Have the two training sessions spaced apart, with perhaps one in the morning and one in the early evening. If morning is not a good time for you, you can practice once in the early evening and once a couple of hours later but not within an hour of "bedtime".

Treats play a huge role in enticing your puppy to follow this command. Therefore, your dog should be hungry when you do these training sessions. However, be sure that he is not starving for dinner as he will be too focused on wanting to devour a full meal and not be able to stay focused. A dog in training should be hungry enough that treats are desired.

While each puppy has his own learning rate, if the training is done as often as described above and in the way that is explained ahead, your puppy may be able to master this command in one to three weeks.

Remember to end on a "high note" when your puppy is doing well. Give praise for "good attempts" and work to keep the morale high. Finally, remember to never say "No" and to say "Uh-oh" instead.

Step-by-Step Instructions

1- Choose a room that has little distractions. You may also wish to do this outside, but again it should be an area with few (or no) distractions.

2- Have a treat in your hand, and also some in your pocket.

3- Have your dog on leash.

4- Stand or kneel right in front of your dog, holding a treat in your hand a little higher than your dog's head.

5- Slowly move the treat straight back over your dog's head. This should cause his nose to point up and his rump to drop down to the floor. If his rump does not drop, keep moving the treat straight backward toward his tail. The very moment that his rump touches the floor, give him the treat and signal the desired behavior by saying, "Good Sit!" in a happy voice.

Note: It is important to say "Good SIT" and not "Good boy" or "Good girl" because saying "Good Sit!" reinforces the command, allowing your dog to have a

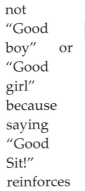

better understanding of why he is being rewarded.

6- Once your dog has shown you that he sits when commanded in this way, move on to the stage of waiting a few seconds before giving him the reward. Remember to only reward while your dog is in the correct position of squarely sitting on the floor. For all attempts, only enthusiastic praise is given to encourage the dog to keep trying.

7- Slowly increase the amount of time that you wish for your dog to sit. Start with just a count of three seconds. When you are ready for him to come out of the "Sit", say "Okay" (the release word). Say it as if you are saying, "You are free!" and use a hand motion to send that message.

When your dog moves out of the sitting position, offer him praise and a pat. Do not offer a treat, but do make it clear that you are happy that he not only sat, but came out of the sit when you released him with the word of "Okay".

Possible Hiccups

If your dog jumps at your hand that is holding the treat: If this happens, hold the treat lower.

If your dog sits, but then keeps getting up before you release him with the "Okay" release word: In a gentle but firm way, keep placing your dog back into a sit. Be sure to not give the treat until he has been in the position for a count of three.

The "Down" Command

You may wonder why "Down" is needed if a dog has already learned to obey "Sit". There are actually some very good reasons. These reasons will especially hold true for a hyper puppy or dog. To have a very well-mannered canine family member, there will be times when "Down" will need to be given.

"Down" is a more firm, serious command than "Sit". While "Sit" is a command given before a dog eats, to put on their leash and for other reasons, "Sit" is not an immediate *need*. While you will want your dog to "Sit" when you command, nothing terrible will occur if hypothetically he did not listen.

However, with "Down", this more serious command will be given for more serious situations. It will be used if your dog is heading toward the street and could be hit by a car...It will be used if your dog is unexpectedly reacting aggressively toward someone.

The "Down" command is useful when you are out in public and in a place that could pose potential dangers. Having your dog immediately go "Down" upon command will allow you to have control. As time goes by, you will use this command and be happy that you taught this to your dog.

The Goal

The goal of this command will be that when the command "Down" is given, your dog will quickly lie down fully, without his rump sticking up; his belly will be flush down onto the floor. He will stay in this position until you give the release word.

What You Should Know About this Command

Since this command is a bit more difficult to master than "Sit", "Sit" should be taught first. Since "Sit'" can be taught as soon as an owner obtains a young eight week old puppy, this command can be taught as early as nine weeks.

Do remember that a dog of any age can learn any command. Therefore, if you have an older dog, he can learn this important command as well. Sessions should last ten to fifteen minutes, done twice per day until the command is mastered. The command should be given at least one time per day (preferably twice) afterward to reinforce the learned behavior.

Treats play a large role in enticing your puppy to follow this command. Therefore, your dog should be hungry when you do these training sessions. However, be sure that your dog is not starving for dinner as he will be too focused on wanting to devour a full meal. He should be hungry enough that the treats are desired.

While each puppy learns at his own rate, if the training is done as often as described above and it is done exactly as described ahead, your puppy may be able to master this command in one to three weeks. Remember to end on a "high note" when your puppy is doing well.

Give praise for "good attempts" and work to keep the morale high. Finally, remember to never say "No" and to say "Uh-oh" instead.

Step-by-Step Instructions

1- Choose a room that has little distractions. You may also wish to do this outside, but again it should be an area with few (or no) distractions.

2- Have a treat in your hand, and also some in your pocket.

3- Have your dog on leash.

4- With your dog facing you, hold a treat to his nose and lower it slowly to the floor. As you do this, say "Down" in a firm voice.

5- In the best case scenario, your dog will simply follow the treat with his nose and lie down. If so, immediately give him the treat and praise him by saying, "Good Down!" Remember to only release the treat while your dog is in the correct position. Do not give it to him if he gets up – that will be too late and he will think that you are rewarding the action of rising up.

If your dog hunches over, slide the treat slowly toward him on the floor between his front paws or away from him. It may take a little time but your dog will ultimately lie down.

6-   Once your dog has shown you that he goes down when commanded in this way, move on to the stage of waiting a few seconds before giving him the reward. Remember to only reward while your dog is in the correct position of being flat on the floor. With your dog in a "Down", say, "Wait...wait" and then "Good Down!" while offering the treat.

7-   After your dog has the treat, release him from the "Down" by saying "Okay!" Say it as if you are saying, "You are free!" and use a hand motion to send that message. When your dog comes out of the down position, offer him praise and a pat. Do not offer a treat, but do make it clear that you are happy that he not only went down, but that he came out of the down when you released him with the command of "Okay".

8-   Once your dog has mastered this, go up to the next stage of ordering "Down" in different situations. You will ultimately want your dog to learn to drop "Down" when outside playing, when walking, when other people are around, etc. if you command for it.

If your dog goes down, but then keeps getting up before you release him with the "Okay" release word: Never offer the treat if he rises up before you say "Okay". Make sure that he sees the treat and try again. Remember the need for patience.

There *will* be a first time that your dog does lie down and when you immediately give him the treat, he will make the connection that a treat is only his when he goes down. Also, re-think your treat, it may need to be more special, such as crisp, crumbled bacon. Any treat that is normally given throughout the day will have no more impact other than for a dog to metaphorically think, "Oh, a bit of food, thank you" and not consider it to be a reward for an action.

Finally, for stubborn dogs, you can place your foot on the leash once the dog is down, which prevents him from being able to fully rise up.

If your dog will obey "Down" in one room of the house, but not in a different one: This often can be caused by different ground textures, for example if the second room has a colder, harder surface. If this is the case, try placing down a blanket or towel until your dog has better mastered obeying this command.

Some owners use "Down" when they really wish to communicate an "Off". "Off" will be used if your dog is sitting atop a chair that you placed your favorite shirt on or another scenario in which you really mean to say, "Move, please!"

The "Stay" Command

Once your dog has learned "Sit" and

"Down", the next logical command to teach him is to "Stay". While you have been teaching "Sit" and "Down" while using the technique of keeping him in position until you give the release word of "Okay", it will now be time to teach your dog that "Stay" is a command that is to be followed, no matter where he is or what position he may be in.

Just like "Down", "Stay" will keep your dog safe. There are so many circumstances in which this will be used. You may be loading groceries out of the car and command "Stay" to your dog so that he does not even try to run around while you are focused on something else.

You may give the "Stay" command if a friend comes over with their own puppy and you want your dog to stay back for a minute while you access the situation. You may be grooming your dog and just as you are about to finish, he gets antsy and therefore commanding "Stay" can allow you the couple of minutes that you need to finish up.

Dogs love to run around and play, especially puppies. Running around is just fine if it is done in a safe area. But since a dog may try to run when you least expect it, "Stay" can allow to you stop him in his tracks.

If you teach your dog to "Stay", this is a huge element of having a well-behaved, well-mannered dog. You will be proud of his behavior and your dog will be proud to receive praise from you and compliments from others for behaving so nicely.

The Goal

The goal of this command will be that when the command "Stay" is given, your dog will remain where he is. If not in a "Sit" or a "Down", he will not freeze in position as if he is a statue; however his footing will remain in place and he will not walk, run or otherwise move from where he is at the time the command is given.

A dog may naturally sit down after stopping and this is fine as the ultimate goal is to have a dog stay where he is whether sitting or standing.

What You Should Know About this Command

While this command is usually taught after "Sit" and "Down" are learned, an owner can begin to teach this command during the other training. In that case, instead of saying, "Wait....wait..." as a dog is in the "Down" position, an owner can use the words "Stay...stay" to help their dog grasp what this word means.

As with most command training, treats play a large role in encouraging your puppy to follow along. Therefore, your dog should be hungry when you do these training sessions. However, be sure that your dog is not starving for dinner as he will be too focused on wanting to devour a full meal. A dog must desire a treat in order for it to be a motivator.

While each puppy learns at his own rate, if the training is done as often as described above and it is done exactly as described ahead, your puppy may be able to master this command in one to three weeks. Remember to end on a "high note" when your puppy is doing well. Give praise for "good attempts" and work to keep the morale high. Finally, remember to never say "No" and to say "Uh-oh" instead.

The tone of your voice and your body language will play a huge role in getting your message across. A dog must see that you are serious when you do this training. This is a more serious order than the "Wait" that you say when teaching "Down". Wait is more of a request; "Stay" is a command.

Step-by-Step Instructions

1- Choose a room that has little distractions. For this command, it is best to first reach success indoors and then move to outdoor training.

2- Have a treat in your hand, and also some in your pocket.

3- Have your dog on leash.

4- Start with your dog in a "Sit" or a "Down", as he will be less apt to move from those positions. As he will be on leash, be sure to hold the end of the leash in your hand.

5- Stand directly in front of him and in a serious tone, command "Stay". When you say "Stay", slowly hold out your hand, palm facing out to your dog, almost close enough to touch his nose.

6- Move a short distance away, keeping eye contact with your dog. As you slowly back up, keep your hand up and say, "Stayyyy" in a tone that implies that you do not want him to move and something is about to happen.

Then, slowly return to him. When you return to him, praise him with "Good Stay!" and give him a treat. Be sure to give the praise and treat while your dog remains in his starting position and has not yet moved. He can move his head and wiggle a bit, as he is not expected to remain frozen, but you will want to offer treat and reward before he moves from the spot.

7- If your dog moves from his stay before you have released him, gently but firmly put him back in the area where he was originally told to stay.

8- As he learns this, gradually increase the time that you ask for your dog to stay, as well as the distance between the two of you.

9- You want your dog to be successful therefore if he is breaking the stay, go back to a time and shorter distance that he is able to achieve and reinforce that for a couple more days before increasing distance or time.

10- After your dog has stayed and you have given the praise of "Good Stay" and have given the reward, release him from the stay by saying "Okay!" Say it as if you are saying, "You are free!" and use a hand motion to send that message. When your dog comes out of the stay position, offer him praise and a hug. Do not offer a treat, but do make it clear that you are happy that he not only stayed in position, but came out of the stay when you released him with the word of "Okay".

Possible Hiccups

If your dog breaks from the stay before you are ready to give him the treat: Do not show him the treat until you give it to him, as it may cause him to pull forward. Fluctuate your pattern, sometimes returning to him and leaving him again without rewarding.

The "Come" Command

If an owner does not teach his or her dog the "Come" command, they can find themselves chasing their dog around a lot of the time. When a dog runs from an owner and that owner runs after them, this creates an atmosphere of chaos and additionally it sends a message that the dog is trying to gain control (be the Alpha) and the human is showing shaky leadership skills by partaking in the game of "chase".

A well-behaved, well-mannered dog will come when called. He may not *want* to stop playing, but he will defer to his leader. It will be important to not even consider asking a dog to "Come" when he is eating. A dog should *never* be bothered in any way when he is consuming a meal and *certainly* not be commanded to leave his dish to "Come" to an owner.

The Goal

The goal of this command will be that when the command "Come" is given, your dog will immediately stop what he is doing and walk or trot over to wherever it is that you are positioned.

He will not necessarily sit or lie down unless you then give that second command. The objective is only to have your dog come over to you and wait for whatever is to happen next, whether that is having his leash put on for a walk or be commanded to "Sit" in order to eat dinner.

What You Should Know About this Command

When you are training your dog to "Come", this command should not be used in order to have your dog come over to you for something that he will consider to be unpleasant. If so, he will be reluctant to learn this. Later, once your dog has mastered this command, you can then use it any time that it is appropriate even for less than delightful tasks such as calling your dog to come over for a nail trimming.

While many owners call out their dog's name when they want him to "Come", commanding "Come" is much more serious than calling out their name. Calling out your dog's name should be a request, but ordering "Come" is a serious "Come over here right now". A dog's name can be added to the command of "Come" such as "Come, Rocko!" The command should be spoken first and *then* the name added if desired.

A dog can learn the meaning of the word very quickly, but practice and reinforcement of this command should continue for life so that a dog never forgets this and you will be able to count on him to come whenever you say the word.

Step-by-Step Instructions

1- Choose a room that has little distractions. You may also wish to practice this outside, as it offers you more room for training; however do try to do it in a place and at a time that offers few (or no) distractions until your dog has moved along in mastering this.

2- Have a treat in your hand, and also some in your pocket.

3- Have your dog on a short, six foot leash. It is highly and strongly recommended to only do this with a harness on him and NOT just a dog collar. With just a collar and not a harness, a dog can be injured during this training.

4- Standing the six foot distance away from your dog (that the leash allows), command your dog to "Come". Sometimes, just the tone of your voice will prompt him to do so. If he does not, persuade him to do so by reeling him in to you at a moderate rate of speed that he can follow along with, as you do not want to be dragging him. Your voice should be happy yet firm.

Give the command word of "Come" only one time as the goal is to have your dog obey with the command only being said one time.

5- As soon as he is over to you, say, "Good Come!" and offer a treat.

6- At this point, immediately give a second command of "Sit" so that he can see that coming over had a purpose. Give reward for the "Sit" and then release with "Okay".

7- As you practice, you will see that your dog will come over to you with little or no action taken on your part of reeling him in by the leash.

8- As you practice a bit more, you will now be able to use longer leashes; increasing the starting distance between you and your dog. Be sure that your dog has mastered one step before moving on to a more challenging one.

9- After your dog is has successfully mastered coming over to you while on leash, it will be time to practice without a leash. This should be done indoors or in a safe, enclosed outdoor area in which your dog is not able to run from the area.

Let the leash be attached, but do not hold onto the other end. If he does not obey your command when you say it one time, go to him and firmly lead him back to the spot where you stood when giving the command. Do not give a reward if your dog does not perform the command on his own, the first time that you say it. Put a long leash back on him. Require him to do five successful "Comes" before attempting this off-leash again.

Possible Hiccups

If your dog runs away when they are off-leash: Do not chase after your dog. If you do, that will only encourage him to keep running as if it is a game. Stay where you are and firmly command that he "Come". If he *still* does not come over, you can nonchalantly walk over to the end of the leash, re-gain your composure and begin again at the lower level of on-leash training.

If he is running around like *silly* and you would need to run after the leash in order to grab hold, it will then be best to *completely* ignore him. When utterly ignored (no talking, no eye contact) a puppy will usually walk over to his owner just to find out why he or she is not paying attention to him. You can then take hold of the end of the leash, re-gain your composure and begin again at the lower level of on-leash training.

 This command should not be given unless you are serious about needing your dog to obey it, willing to put him on leash to force him to obey it if necessary. If you are not in a position to carry it out, do not give the command. Instead, just call your dog's name or use "Here Boy" or "Here Girl", which is more of a request that will not

be detrimental to this training if he or she does not listen to you.

"Shake My Hand" – Teaching Your Dog to Greet People Nicely

Unlike the previous "Sit", "Stay", "Down" and "Come", this "command" and the following are more "tricks" than commands.

They are not needed in the same way as the others are. During the daily routine of taking care of your dog, you will want him to sit and stay, come to you and lie down for various legitimate reasons.

"Shake my hand", is not a necessary command for a dog, but it is a nice additional element for having a well-behaved, well-trained dog. It is wonderful if your dog goes beyond the basics and learns to interact with you and others in this way.

When a dog not only obeys basic, serious commands but additionally obeys "requests" that are amusing, this is an outward symbol a canine's intelligence. It allows an owner to have a dog that he can show off. The dog is poised and ready to display his skills at any time. Therefore, this leads to an overall representation of having a dog that is not only well-trained, but also a dog that is entertaining, displays his friendly qualities and is fun to be around.

The Goal

When shaking hands, your dog will raise his paw to his chest height allowing you or others to shake his paw.

What You Should Know About this Command

Just like humans, dogs are right handed, left handed or ambidextrous (using both front paws in an equal way). Therefore, most dogs will favor one paw over the other. While a dog can be taught to use both paws for this, it is best to allow your dog to use whichever paw he seems to be more comfortable with. Since his paw and your hand will not interlock, it will have no effect on this trick if he raises his left or his right paw.

Step-by-Step Instructions

1- Choose a room that has little distractions. Since the outdoors often has more distractions than inside, it often best to practice inside and then only moving outside once your dog is on his way to mastering this.

2- Have a treat in your right hand (or your left hand if you are left handed), and also some in your pocket.

3- Command your dog to "Sit".

4- Once he is sitting, lower your hand that is holding the treat, bringing it down close to the ground.

5- Encourage your dog to paw at your hand by allowing him to see the treat and moving it around. Say the word, "Shake" or the phrase "Shake my hand" if preferred – with emphasis on the word "Shake".

6- Many dogs will nose at the hand instead of pawing it. If your dog does sniff at it, ignore this and do not release the treat. He may try barking, nuzzling or he may do nothing at all. Be patient, and keep encouraging him. If he is not moving his paw on his own, you can lift it for him to touch your hand and then reward...If this is the case, each time you do this, gradually using less and less force to lift it, as he learns to raise it on his own.

7- Reward your dog with the treat the moment his paw comes off of the floor and moves toward your hand, saying "Good Shake!" even if the paw raises just a bit, as it is important to praise and reward "attempts" as your dog learns this challenging trick.

8- Gradually raise the height of your hand as you progress, until he is lifting his paw to his chest height.

9- Once your dog is progressing well, move on to the next step of standing up and holding the treat in your left hand, behind your back. Bend down to whatever level is appropriate to "shake hands" with your dog. Put out your right hand and give the command of "Shake" or "Shake my hand" (whichever you have been using). If your dog does indeed raise his paw to meet your hand, immediately say "Good Shake!" and offer him the treat.

Once your dog has mastered this trick, to add a nice finishing touch to this training in order to create an amusing exchange of saying hello, you can then move on to saying, "How are you?" or any other comment after the shake instead of the "Good Shake" reply (that was needed during training for reinforcement) and giving a treat as you say those words. After a couple of months (or even less in some cases), no treat will be needed as a dog's movements become automated upon hearing the command word.

The "Give that to Me" Command

Once your dog has mastered this, he will hand over an object to you when you request it (and by "hand over", *"mouth over"* is what is technically meant!). When a dog does this it shows that he is very well-mannered and well trained. There will be no chasing your dog around the house to retrieve an object that he has mouthed. If he mouths something that you do not want him chewing on, he will hand it over to you upon your request.

Many owners have found this to be literally lifesaving, when their dog had an element in his mouth that would have been toxic upon swallowing (batteries are most common).

Finally, it is a nice command for a dog to learn as it creates a relationship in which your dog listens to you when you politely ask for something.

When you begin training for this, your voice will be serious, firm and encouraging. Once your dog follows this command due to his body's automated reaction to hearing the word(s), your voice can be more relaxed and polite.

Importantly, when a dog learns this command, it confirms that he sees you as the Alpha. As discussed earlier, when a dog has a very clear understanding that his human is the leader, this shapes his personality. The dog is at peace that he does not have the pressure of leading the pack and he behaves better in all situations than he would otherwise.

The Goal

Upon an owner saying the "Give it to me" command, a dog will release an object from his mouth, directly into the owner's hand.

What You Should Know About this Command

For this command, training at the beginner level will involve returning an object to your dog. The advance level will involve *not* returning the object. Therefore, when you are ready to begin training, your dog will either have a food element returned to him or a toy returned to him. If he is attached to one element very strongly and therefore resists following the command, you may find that it is the other element that will work best for this.

If you choose "food", it will be a snack, perhaps a rawhide that he chews on that takes several days to fully consume; it will not be food that is placed into his bowl for meals.

For example purposes, as you read the instructions for this command training, the word "rawhide" will be used; if you have chosen to do this training with a toy, "toy" can be replaced with "rawhide".

Commands are always short words, since a dog often only pays attention to the first word of a sentence or the first strong sounding syllable. Therefore, you will say, "GIVE that to me, please," with a strong emphasis on the word "give".

When your dog obeys this command, he will do so when hearing the word "Give" while you will be adding the "that to me, please" to produce a more polite "request" that he listens to as opposed to an otherwise stern and harsh sounding command of only "Give". Once he has mastered this command, you will be able to say the word "Give" in a normal voice and not emphasized.

Step-by-Step Instructions

1- Have a special treat in your hand, keeping your hand cupped.

2- When your dog has the rawhide in his mouth, say the command of "Give that to me" while placing *strong* verbal emphasis on the word "Give" as you hold out your hand (the one that is not cupping the treat).

3- Do not move from your position and keep repeating the command until your dog offers it to you. It may take several minutes, but when your dog finally mouths the rawhide into your free hand, say "Good Give!" and reward him by offering the treat and then by giving him his rawhide back.

It will be important to give the rawhide back immediately after he swallows the treat, as he must understand that when he gives it to you, you give it right back.

4- As your dog progresses, allow for longer periods of time in which you hold onto the rawhide. Do give the treat right away, but as each day goes on, add seconds to time that passes before he is given his rawhide back.

5- Once your dog has mastered giving you something that he really wanted (to have it returned to him relatively soon) it will be time to move onto other objects. These will be objects that he will not mind if they are not returned to him, as long as he receives his treat.

Training for this can be spontaneous when your dog randomly mouths an object, so keep your eyes out for this. You can also encourage him to mouth an object (such as the newspaper or remote) that you wish to have him routinely bring to you. Begin by always offering a treat for reward…As this becomes an automated response, offer a treat every other time…and then finally just your praise will be enough to instill this command.

If your dog will not give the object to you: Try practicing this command when he is mouthing a different object. If you do this when he has his *favorite* toy, he *may* be much too attached to want to give it up to you, even if a treat a reward for doing so. If you do this with a less loved toy or chew, he will be more prone to follow along.

Never try to force the object from your dog's mouth as it can cause injury.

The "Let's Talk" Command & The Wonderful "Whisper"

While this command is not "needed" as a basic foundation for a well-behaved dog, it is a delightful addition to learned skills that a dog can have. When a dog acquires this talent, it creates true  verbal interaction between human and canine. Many owners teach this command by saying "Speak!" however it is suggested to use the words "Let's Talk" since this creates a nice exchange: You will say (actually command) "Let's Talk" and your dog will respond to you by "talking" (actually barking upon command).

Only teach this command to your dog if he is not prone to excessive barking; if your dog is going through a barking phase (something that socialization training can fix) it will be best to wait before you encourage any more barking.

The Goal

Your dog will bark one time, on cue. It will not be endless barking that then needs to be controlled. It will be a bark that gives the appearance that your dog is truly "speaking" when asked to.

What You Should Know About this Command

For this command to work an owner must first identify a trigger; it will be something that normally causes the dog to bark. If a dog has a strong trigger, such as barking when the doorbell rings, this command can be learned rather quickly, sometimes within just one week.

It may take some time to find a trigger that causes your dog to bark as each dog is different. For owners who cannot find a trigger, what then often works best is to create one. One easy design is to put pennies into a metal can; when shaken, this can prompt a dog to bark.

It will be important to use a trigger that you never plan on teaching your dog to *not* bark at. If so, this would cause great confusion as a dog cannot be told to bark and not bark at the same element.

Since many dogs do bark when a can filled with pennies is shaken, this will be used as an example for the training instructions. As with all training, do remember that once your dog has mastered this, you will need to routinely say the command to make sure that your dog has not forgotten his training.

Step-by-Step Instructions

1- Begin training in a room that has very few (or no distractions)

2- -Keep a treat in your hand, cupped so that your dog does not focus on it.

3- Shake the can while giving the command of "Let's Talk!"

4- As soon as your dog barks, stop shaking the can and immediately say "*Good*, Let's Talk!" and give him the treat. It will be very important to give him the treat after as little as one bark since you do not want to teach your dog "barking", you only want to teach him to let out *one* bark.

5- You may need to shake the can, pause and shake it again several times in order for your dog to bark.

6- A truly wonderful addition to this training is to build on this to include a "Whisper". This can only be taught once a dog has learned "Let's Talk". Training your dog to whisper is done by using the command of "Let's Talk, but Whisper", with strong emphasis on the word "whisper". The command will be, "*Let's talk, but WHISPER!*" said in a hushed tone, while your pointer finger raises to your lips.

Only praise with *"Good Whisper!"* (Also said in a hushed tone of voice) and reward with a treat with your dog produces a lower volume bark than his normal bark. If your dog barks at normal volume, do not give the treat; simply repeat the command in the hushed tone, emphasis on the "whisper" and with your finger pressed to your lips.

If you simply cannot find a trigger that causes your dog to bark: If your dog is very easy going, and nothing prompts him to bark, teasing him just a bit may work. Many dogs will let out a bark if they are feeling just a bit frustrated. In this case, show your dog a treat, but withhold it and tease him a bit by saying, "Do you want it... Do you?....*Let's Talk!*" If your dog then barks, immediately say, "Good, Let's Talk!" and give him the treat.

Never reward your dog for a bark unless you asked for the bark by saying "Let's Talk".

Breaking the Begging Behavior

When a puppy or dog is always begging for some of their owner's food, this behavior was often created at the very moment when an owner first performed the simple act of innocently giving the dog one tiny morsel of human food. Many owners do not think twice about it. If your dog relentlessly begs for food, it is most likely because this one seemingly harmless action of handing a piece of your food to your dog started a behavioral issue that may appear to grow stronger each day.

A dog that is given his owner's food just *one* time thinks the equivalent of, ""If I was given my owner's food once, I'm positive that I can have it again, I just need to *keep* begging for it!"

So how can you stop your dog from begging? Training to end this type of behavior will take strict discipline; some owners have a difficult time sticking with this as they feel bad for their dog. However one must remember that many human foods are not only unhealthy for dogs, some are downright toxic.

One example is onions which can be found in pizza sauce and many other meals without a human even noticing. Depending on the size of your puppy or dog, ingesting just a bit of onion can trigger a severe reaction.

 The top foods that are toxic to canines are: chocolate, coffee, grapes, raisins, macadamia nuts, onions, apple seeds, peach pits, plum pits and yeast dough.

Additionally, if you wish to have a well-trained, well-behaved dog, begging behavior has no place in this. A begging dog can be mentally wearing on an owner; they may find that they spend a large portion of time putting effort into trying to handle this issue. If an owner chooses to train a dog to stop begging, while time and effort will need to be put forth during the training, once it is complete the owner must never deal with this issue again.

You must be consistent and non-wavering. Once you prove to your dog that begging is counter-productive and life is not fun when he is begging, your dog will stop.

How do you do this? Social isolation is the key, which is the equivalent of being temporarily "banned from the pack". Before you take this on, if there are other human family members beside yourself in the home, it is suggested to hold a family meeting. Discuss that you will all need to work together as a team to train your dog to stop begging for food. Make sure that everyone understand the rules of this training and that everyone agrees to follow the rules 100% of the time, no matter how much your dog begs.

This type of training will take several weeks and you may need to maintain a high level of patience. However keep in mind that when you are done, you will have a well behaved dog. You will have a dog that is polite when company comes over for dinner and you will have a canine family member that lets you eat in peace...both elements that are worth a few weeks of training!

The key is to 100% *completely and absolutely* ignore your dog when he is begging for your food. Now, this does not mean that you are just to not give your dog your food. This means that as your dog howls, barks, jumps, whines, begs and makes those "puppy dog eyes", you must act as if he is invisible and you cannot hear him.

If anyone gives in and at any point in the day offers human food to your dog, training must begin all over again from the beginning. So it is very important to stick to this training method without fail.

It is best if you plan to have your dog's dinner time be the same time as your dinner time. This is recommended at any rate in order to establish yourself as the Alpha. Following proper feeding guidelines, you will eat for at least 30 seconds, rise from the table to command your dog to sit and then after he does so, you will set down his dog food and then proceed back to the dinner table. Expect it to be a very noisy dinnertime for the first couple of weeks as your dog makes every sound possible to gain your attention.

Whenever your dog displays begging behavior every human in the home must 100% fully and utterly ignore him. This means no eye contact, no touching and no talking. It is recommended to even keep discussions between humans to a minimum so that the dog does not confuse this for being spoken to. Everyone must stay relaxed and eat his or her own meals. Remember, while your dog will be causing a commotion, your job is to pretend that he is invisible.

If your dog jumps up and physically bothers you, it will be best to leash him away from the human food. (Be sure to use a *harness* and not a collar on puppies, as most will be jumping *up and out* during this time). Keep your dog within sight and do *not* put your dog outside or into another room. Why? Because if your dog does not see the food and has the chance to beg for it, he will not learn that begging is an unacceptable behavior.

Your dog needs to be in the situation of human food being near him in order to learn that begging for it will not be beneficial to him.

If at any time, your dog stops begging and sits or remains still for a count of ten, it is very important to praise him. During this initial training period, you will want to *over-praise* your dog. Say "Good Dog" several times in a tone that implies that you are very happy and proud of him.

Whether your dog is sitting or lying down, get to his level and gently pat him. Do not take action that will cause him to become all excited, but let it be very clear that you approve of his behavior. Do *not* give a treat as you do not want to give the message that begging and then being quiet for a short while produces a treat being handed to him.

As time moves on, your dog will reach a point of realizing that begging gets him nowhere and that being ignored is certainly not fun. A dog will learn that when he is quiet, he receives attention and praise. Since a temporary banishment from the "pack" is simply not acceptable to a canine, a dog will then choose the behavior that is most beneficial to him. As he learns this, he will reach a point of refraining from begging for your entire meal.

Whenever your dog shows zero begging behavior during an *entire* meal, give him an extra special reward once everyone is done eating (Just don't have that reward be your food!) During the first few weeks, a dog should also be given a new toy if he does not beg for an *entire* meal.

For those on a budget (and who is not these days!) there are "dollar stores" in many locations at which you can purchase dog toys very inexpensively...Just be sure to check each toy so that you feel confident that it is safe to play with.

When your dog has remained quiet during your entire meal, give great words of praise and pats. If your dog loves attention, spend some time throwing a ball around or another activity that he loves to do. It is very important that your dog learns that when he behaves, life is much better!

Having a Dog that is a Welcomed Member of the Community

Unless you live in a remote location, you will have neighbors. The training that you have read so far has taught your dog to behave very well for you, the family and when with you outside of the home. You have trained your dog to listen to commands, walk nicely beside you and do as you ask. Aside from this, when you follow a few easy guidelines, you can have a dog that is seen by neighbors as being a delight.

Most of us, at one time or another, have had a neighbor with a pet that we were not pleased with. Perhaps you lived next door to someone who owned a dog that barked endlessly or rummaged through your trash cans. Or maybe you have resided in a neighborhood where a dog was allowed to roam the streets, as a possible threat to other dogs and to young children.

While your dog is part of your family and you must live a lifestyle that suits you; to have your dog perceived as being a good neighbor and a welcomed member of the community, a dog owner should be considerate to those living around them. Whether you live in an apartment building or a house, there are a few steps that you can take so that everyone considers your dog to a pleasure to live next to. While you may not be able to appease those who dislike dogs, following these tips show that you are implementing proper etiquette for those living around you.

These steps also include elements that all owners should follow to properly care for their dog by providing a safe and loving environment.

Running Loose

Allowing a dog to run loose can actually affect your neighbor's emotional health and how they view you, your family and your dog. While you may *know* that your dog is not going to bite anyone, others may not have that same reassurance.

In a United States poll, 31% of people disclosed that they are wary of dogs, and this includes all breeds of dogs, even toy and small breed dogs. Of those people, 17% had strong phobias that caused an uncontrollable fear when seeing a loose dog. Therefore, even a very friendly dog that is off-leash can create a feeling of uneasiness in a person and even deep distress.

Not allowing your dog to run loose also keeps him safe. Broken limbs are among the top 5 emergency reasons a dog is rushed to the veterinarian and this is most often due to being hit by a car. If left unattended outside, a dog can chew on toxic grasses, weeds and flowers. Male dogs that are un-neutered often chase after female dogs in heat. And female dogs that are in heat are in danger of un-neutered male dogs that can injure them.

Another possible dreadful outcome of having your dog running around is that a neighbor may call an animal shelter to pick up your dog. Some overloaded animal shelters will euthanize a dog within three short days if he is not claimed. For all of these reasons, it is highly suggested to keep your dog on leash or in a safe, enclosed yard.

Elimination All Over the Neighborhood

No one wants to sidestep dog feces when they are walking in their neighborhood. If your dog is leaving behind feces around the community, your neighbors are most likely going to know who the culprit was and they will not appreciate it. Additionally, when you are housetraining your dog, you will want him to go to the bathroom in the designated area and not when walking, as described in the previous "Housetraining" chapter.

If you will be going for a long walk it is a good idea to bring along a "dog waste bag" to scoop up any feces, should your dog have a bowel movement along the way. These bags can be bought in bulk and are relatively inexpensive. Many states and regions have local laws that decree a dog owner must pick up and dispose of their dog's bowel movements. Even if your area does not have this local law, for your dog to be a good neighbor and a welcomed member of the community, it is suggested to do this.

If you are walking your dog in your neighborhood and he appears to need to eliminate, do not allow him to do so in anyone's yard. Let your dog take care of business in an area that does not appear to receive foot traffic when at all possible and then scoop it up with the bag.

The Polite Dog

Just as we expect our human neighbors to be courteous, it is a pleasure when a dog neighbor is polite as well. This is an integral part of socializing your dog. If your dog jumps on your neighbors, barks or behaves badly, this can be corrected with socialization training. If your goal is to have your dog perceived as a pleasure to be around as opposed to being a nuisance, following a few simple yet important steps will ensure this.

Having your dog fully know the basic commands of sit, stay, come, down and heel will control any jumping or overactive behavior. Teaching your dog to never "play bite" with people is encouraged.

A dog should not "take over" a room or a piece of furniture if a human wishes to sit down upon it. If you have visitors and your dog wants the sofa, teach him that it is polite to allow visitors to sit there. You can do this by calling your dog to you, commanding him into a "Sit" or "Down" and then offering him a treat or toy. Have the visitors sit on the sofa and praise your dog for behaving nicely.

Exposing your dog to a variety of other dogs, pets and people will allow your dog to become accustomed to all sorts of elements and after a while your dog will not overreact in situations. Proper socialization is a gradual process which includes both the introduction to elements and teaching the appropriate response. Having your dog in the company of others for a short amount of time and slowly progressing to longer increments is the best method. Over-stimulation often only makes things worse.

Following these tips will ensure that most (if not all) of your neighbors will welcome the sight of your canine family member and come to appreciate him for the wonderful, loving dog that he is.

Other books by Faye Dunningham
(Found on Amazon!)

The Well Socialized Dog: Step-by-Step Socialization Training for Puppies and Dogs

Chewing, Tugging, Nipping and Biting: Detailed Step-by-Step Training and Care for Puppies and Dogs

Made in the USA
Lexington, KY
18 December 2012